I Close My Eyes To Breathe

Unlearning Survival, Becoming Whole: A Guide to Healing, Self-Love, and Emotional Wellness

Shaaree McCalpine

Faith Soars Publishing

ISBNs
Paperback: 979-8-9957521-0-3
eBook: 979-8-9957521-1-0
Hardback: 979-8-9957521-2-7

Published by **Faith Soars Publishing**
Canton, Michigan
www.faithsoarscounseling.com

Scripture Credits
Unless otherwise indicated, all scripture quotations are taken from the Holy Bible.

First Edition
Printed in the United States of America

For bulk orders, speaking engagements, or workshop inquiries, visit our website. For permissions or other inquiries, contact the publisher.

A Guide to Healing, Self-Love and Emotional Wellness

This book was created for the woman who has learned to survive but is ready for something more—more peace, more clarity, more wholeness.

It is a space to pause, reflect, and begin again, on your terms.

Inside these pages, you will be invited to:

- Release survival habits that no longer serve you

- Rebuild trust, boundaries, and emotional safety within yourself

- Reconnect with your needs, your voice, and your peace

SHAAREE MCCALPINE, MA, MBA, LPC

A licensed therapist, speaker, author, and founder of Faith Soars Counseling and Consultation. Since 2012, her work has been rooted in one mission: creating spaces where women can finally exhale.

Through her practice, Shaaree has walked alongside women carrying the quiet weight of daily pressures, guiding them toward healing, wholeness, and hope. Her approach blends clinical expertise with faith, compassion, and real-life understanding.

I Close My Eyes to Breathe is an extension of that work. It's more than a book, it's a conversation. A safe space. A reminder that you are seen, supported, and still becoming.

Dedication

To little Shaaree from grown up Shar

To Tailour who is growing in purpose, passion, and understanding of herself.

To Paiton who is stepping into curiosity, possibilities, blessings, and greatness.

To Brandon, who is learning what greatness and growth looks like.

To Brandon Jr. who is growing with wonder, love, and strength.

To all my sisters who have had doubts, struggled, believed in strength but equateding it to struggle, who have cried and had nowhere to put the pain. This is my love letter and heart to you. Grow in the knowledge that you are not broken, you are not "extra" or "too much". You are growing into who YOU were always meant to be. Believing in the promise that, "all things are possible through Christ who strengthens you" (Philippians 4:13). We weren't always taught how to be, but we can change that with tools, compassion, and love.

Contents

Letter to the Reader

Sis, this book was written with you, the Black woman, in mind. You, who has carried so much, given so much, and yet often feels unseen. I Close My Eyes to Breathe is both a mirror and a map. A mirror because you will see yourself, your struggles, and your strength reflected in these pages. A map because it will guide you from survival mode to thriving. Using the framework of Maslow's Hierarchy of Needs and John Bowlby's Attachment Theory, life skills are taught, but in our language, through our stories, in a way that feels real, not like a lecture. This is a book for the woman who's tired of the endless hustle, who feels the weight of expectations, and who secretly wonders, "When is it my turn to breathe?" Inside these pages, you'll meet Keischa and other women whose stories mirror our own. Their voices and journeys will lead us into the heart of what it means to reclaim our peace, rebuild trust with ourselves, set boundaries, and rediscover love—not just romantic love, but self-love, and community love. At the end of each chapter, you'll find reflections, affirmations, and guided exercises. This is not busy work. They're intentional, evidence-based practices designed to give you real tools for your mental, emotional, and spiritual healing. Take your time with them, sis. There's no deadline, no "right way" to complete the exercises. Healing isn't a race, it's a journey. Every reflection, every pause, every breath you take while working through these pages is part of laying a new foundation for yourself. The goal isn't perfection, it's wholeness. Think of this book as your seat at the table with your healing bestie, me, where we laugh, cry, tell the truth, and hold each other accountable to becoming our best selves. This is about more than just surviving. It's about stepping into the full, radiant version of your self-actualized self.So, go slowly. Go with love. And above all, give yourself permission to keep coming back because every time you open these pages, you are choosing yourself.

With love and prayers that Keisha's journey makes a difference,
Shar

Introduction

Life can take you through many twists and turns, but if you listen carefully and do the work you will recognize your behaviors, patterns, and stressors. Listen Sis, no truer statement has been made than, "Life be life-in'." I'm literally laughing out loud at this life I've been given. This life which has taken me through all its peaks and valleys, storms, floods, rainbows and gifts has flooded me with pain, joy, happiness, loneliness, and every emotion in between. Here's the one thing I know for certain; when God gives you another day, take the opportunity to listen, reflect, and decide to think to yourself, maybe I can change, just maybe there is something better and make the decision to take the road of "maybe and decide to think to yourself, maybe I can change, just maybe there is something better.

It's raining. I'm sitting on the porch staring at the ultimate beauty of the sheets of water, listening to the peaceful sounds and declaring the gratitude I have for this moment. It sounds like the trees are whispering and I feel comforted by the wind blowing through them. It's quite mesmerizing. I've always felt connected to trees, so it was by no coincidence I ended up living on a street lined with beautiful trees and foliage.

According to Psalms 1:3 it says, "And he shall be like a tree planted by the rivers of the water, that bringeth forth his fruit in his season; his leaf also shall not wither; and whatsoever he doeth shall prosper." Jeremiah 17:7-8 continues to compare the faithful person to trees planted by water. Listen, my dear sister, I know my audience and at this point y'all like, "Girl, what's with the tree talk?!" I know, I know, stay with me for a minute. It will make sense, and you will see how it relates to us and life.

Trees do a fascinating thing; they grow upward and downward at the same time. Two directions at the same time which is a powerful metaphor about life. We as human beings live life in a duality where two things can exist at the same time and be true. Much like trees, our growth downward anchors us through what we were taught, what we saw, and our developing core memories. Our roots. We learn love and security by how we are connected to our parents, grandparents, and caregivers.

Our growth upwards, our everyday life, our existence, is what we learned, what we believe, what we experience. The experiences that gave us positive fuzzy feelings and the interactions that taught us to shrink back because it wasn't safe to be your authentic self. We got these clues and behaviors from trusted members of our community (teachers, friends, and experts) that said you are better off fitting in than standing out and standing alone.

We learned that it's comfortable to be in safety that safety shields the hurt. It's the growth of the leaves and fruit that needs nourishment, water, and sun to grow. We need those things in order to thrive and grow, but here's the part that's transformative: unlike the beautiful trees, dear soul, we aren't stuck. So, our life and story are endless with tons of possibilities.

If you picked up this book, sugar pies, I know something in you is trying to connect to what's next, to feel a stirring, to change and get the question answered: "How can I move forward?" If you have sat alone in tears wondering what your next move was or silently repeated the thought in your head, "I'm tired, just tired, but what else can I do?" Or you've thought to yourself, "There has got to be something better than this." You have the right book, at the right, and the right friend in me.

There's a quiet exhaustion many Black women know too well – that ache in the chest that comes from holding it all together. We've been told to be strong for so long that we've forgotten, if we ever knew, what softness feels like. We've learned to push through pain, smile through struggle, and succeed through exhaustion. But this book, *I Close My Eyes to Breathe*, is your permission slip to stop performing and start practicing healing and self-love.

This is not another self-help manual written from the outside looking in. This is a healing guide, a mirror, and a safe space. It's written from within the lived experiences of what it means to be a Black woman trying to find herself beneath the layers of expectation, resilience, and survival. Together, we're going to unpack what it means to move from simply existing to fully living guided by Maslow's Hierarchy of Needs and Attachment Theory. These frameworks aren't just psychology, they're the language of our unmet needs, our love wounds, and our path to wholeness.

How to Use this Book

Take your time with this book. There's no timeline for healing. I literally hate it when someone says in a negative way, "Dang, you've been in therapy for a year." Ma'am, our concept of time is misconstrued. Having a therapy session for 55 minutes once a week does not equate to a year. We think of time in segments, but in healing and exploration time is defined by a different trajectory: growth and need.

You aren't on a timeline. However, even knowing this, we don't allow self-permission to do whatever we need for ourselves. If it takes a year to let yourself settle into what you need and value, that is okay. It took way longer than a year to get here.

Each chapter includes reflection prompts, self-work activities, and coping tools that build on one another – much like climbing the layers of Maslow's Hierarchy from safety and love to belonging and self-actualization. These exercises are not homework; they're heart work.

You can spend a week, a month, or even longer on a single chapter. The goal is not speed, it's depth, it's understanding, Sis, it's love. When you give yourself permission to slow down, you'll notice small shifts. The kind of shifts that whisper before they roar.

Use this book as your companion on quiet mornings or long nights when your mind won't rest. Journal your answers, pause when it gets heavy, and come back when you're ready. Healing is not a straight line. It's a circle of returning, learning, reflecting and becoming.

Why This Matters

Right now, I don't even know if I want to say "right now". Let's just say...Black women have been boots-on-the-ground surviving in the middle of our mental health crisis. Been there helping correct and connect, been leaned on for support, and been a team player for generations. The unspoken trauma, the pressure to excel, and the cultural expectation to be "strong" has left many of us running on empty. The hustle-and-grind mentality may have helped us survive, but it's not built for thriving, enjoying and sustaining joy, wealth, and happiness.

This book is your invitation to choose you. Not as an act of selfishness, but as a declaration of worthiness. Healing is your birthright. You don't have to earn peace by suffering for it. You only have to decide you deserve it. So, as you turn these pages take a deep breath and release the weight you've been carrying. At least for now. You are safe here. You are seen. You are not alone.

I'm emotionally connected to you, my reader, my sister, and my own reflection. To think of the years I wasted believing what I was told, caring what others thought. And the fear, oh my God, the fear. The perceptions and fear of this elusive, but much talked about, security that comes with fitting in and trying to belong. As I begin to type, I hear myself singing in my Anita Baker voice, "365 days of the year of wasted time". Lol those aren't the actual words, but the tune was in my head, so there's that.

What I intend to do in this book is give you what we, what I, desperately need: tools and examples of how life can be and what that change can produce. I intend to give you the understanding that you are not alone in your reality and that when thoughts, environments, and exposure change, your life changes.

We are waking up the desires you had when you were a kid. The fearless you that was always in hot pursuit of trying, learning, laughing and not giving a hoot. If you fell, you just got up and did it again. Somewhere along the line you lost the tenacity of trying again, using your imagination to name what the cloud shapes looked like, and running as fast as you could to absolutely no destination. Start to rewind. Remember what made, or makes, you smile. We left our little mini-mes behind, but she is forever there and constantly calling out, "Hey you forgot me!" That little girl is in you, and with you, whether you choose to ignore her or not.

Ok, phew! We got that out the way. Let's get ready to dig in. This book will give you practical tips to move you from an insecure existence to an *I'm ready to move into my best life* experience. Someone said it is with total arrogance that we live our lives as if we have time. What are you going to do with the time you have right here and right now? My dear, let's get ready to reintroduce you: the new, best version of you.

Disclaimer

Disclaimer: This book isn't to give licensed mental health advice. It is for educational and informational purposes only. I am not your therapist. This work is not a replacement for professional mental health services or religious councils. Please seek a dope, amazing, professional therapist and/or religious professional to take you further on your journey.

Chapter One

It All Started with..

"Caring for myself is not self-indulgence, it is self-preservation and that is an act of political warfare." – Audrey Lourde

Ok, cool. Since you are here, I know that y'all are my peeps. Let me start off by letting you know, I'm grateful, humbled, and real talk, feel like you and I are ready for this transformational journey. Let's get into this thing of "being ready." It can, and has, gotten us caught up. Because, let's face it, at times "being ready" implies that we have control, that we got our shit together, and that we are prepared for the future "what ifs". This can be far from the truth. "Being ready", or the illusion of being ready, can bring up a sense of fear, doubt, and insecurity. Because for real for real, when, I ask, are we ever really ready for anything?

Well, because you are still here, I know that you are as close to being ready for change as possible. You picked up this book, even though you don't know if you have the capacity to do one more thing. One more thing added to your growing "To Do List". Buuuuutt because you are still reading, I know you are ready. I understand that you want help getting to a place that answers "the question". The question that we have all asked at one point in our lives: the "There must be more to living than this?!" question. And the "How did I get here?" question. Both are reflections, unanswered longings, and prayers rather than actual questions.

I know all too well what it feels like to be drained, tired, and mentally exhausted. But not from the day-in day-out routine, but the desires that go unfulfilled, unmet, and unanswered. The desires and needs that keep living in your mind and heart, but seem out of reach or too late to go after.

Or the dreaded "after this" mentality takes hold. "After I finish school... after the kids move out...after I find a man." You get it. The "Imma put this on hold and stay in my same old story" story.

We sometimes simply give up because the knowledge isn't there, and we don't know how to make it happen. We are performative and routine based, so the day-to-day struggle can be completed in our sleep. It's normalized and that struggle becomes part of our story or narrative. We become exhausted by the constant tugging of being needed, it's the "I'm so tired of having to do this alone with no help", and the juggling of what needs to be done daily. We become exhausted from thinking of how to balance our lives and make everything work while still participating in a social life. Shoot, a life period. If that's even a thing at this point. Listen, sis, we have all had days when we literally couldn't get out of the car to walk a few feet to the front door.

There's this thing we do of sitting in the car in solitude, silencing the world, closing our eyes to simply catch our breath and de-stress that has become a space of quiet luxury for us. However, even these moments that we allow ourselves to be still, are fleeting. We quickly will ourselves to face it. Whatever "it" is (kids, more work, cooking, relationships, loneliness) on the other side of the waiting door. We give ourselves a pep talk, "Ok girl, take a minute and let's go on in." Even in these moments, we don't allow ourselves me-time because it feels like we are cheating on our responsibilities. Or we have that haunting feeling that it's wrong to sit and do nothing when we know someone or something needs our attention.

Before we go any further, I want you to meet Keischa. Keischa is every woman who's ever carried too much and said, "I'm fine," when she wasn't. She's 36, a mother, a professional, the friend who always shows up, the one who never lets her mask slip. Her life looks put together from the outside, but her body tells another story. Tight shoulders, restless sleep, a chest that never quite expands all the way. She's been surviving so long that rest feels unsafe. What is rest, anyway? It's not familiar or attainable to Keischa.

Keischa's story isn't just hers. It's ours. It's mine. It's our daughters and the generations before us. Through her eyes, her stories, her life you'll see the emotional cost of strength and the quiet courage it takes to let go. You'll follow her as she begins to unlearn the habits of survival. We move through the process of life as she edges toward therapy, toward community, and finally, toward herself.

You'll recognize parts of your own story in her pauses, her flashbacks, her resistance to being still. She becomes the thread that connects the chapters. A living, breathing reflection of what it looks like when a Black woman finally decides she deserves more. That despite what she was taught, she gets to decide what "more" looks like and begins to heal a hurt that she never knew was hers to overcome. To decide that choosing herself isn't an option, it's a necessity for becoming who she is truly meant to be.

Meet Keischa

Keischa was already overwhelmed at 6:00 in the morning. She was getting ready for work, getting the kids ready, looking for this shoe, or that, or the other thing. She was trying to find her keys when her cell phone, or what felt more like a tether, rang. It was chaos in the house, and it was chaos in her mind. She hated that she reflexively answered the call. Her immediate thought was, "Why did I answer?" It was, of course, a family member needing a "quick favor" that wasn't quick or a favor. Keisha felt annoyed. Her heart instantly sank and her face turned red. She didn't say "no" to this person even though she didn't have time, didn't want to do the favor, and knows that this person never offers to help her in return. "So disrespectful," she thought, "but why didn't I say NO?"

Her already racing mind kept replaying the thought, "Why did I do this to myself?" Her chest felt heavy and her thoughts were spinning as she was startled back to the routine of her life by a glass breaking. Keischa sighed heavily. "Another day," she said to no one in particular then dragged herself and the kids out the house to live the same day she had been living over and over. "One thing for sure," Keisha thought. "I know for a fact I'm not living. I'm enduring. I'm surviving." The reality hit her at once, but the honest truth was, she didn't know the difference anymore.

Let's talk about survival mode. You know the feeling: the constant juggling act, the endless giving, the pain of feeling invisible even as you hold everything together. For Black women survival mode isn't just a phase, it is inherited. It's taught. It's learned. It's in the lessons we never asked for.

Who's heard the mantras: "If you put yourself first, you're selfish."

"Be strong, no matter how much it hurts."

"My mom did it and she is the strongest person I know."

"Keep going, because no one's coming to save you"?

It's so ingrained in us that we wear the words like a second skin, like a badge of honor, like a cape that covers us and hides us. But here's the truth no one wants to say out loud, survival mode will kill you slowly. Take a few minutes to think about the act of choosing yourself, of resting, of saying "no", of reclaiming your joy, or being happy as revolutionary.

In a world that thrives on you playing small, being tired, and silent it can be exhausting to fight the battle every day to be seen. It has become the norm, but what happens when you're too exhausted to choose yourself? After so many years of being who you were told you were, taught you were, thought you were, how do you even choose yourself? At this point, you ask the question, "Who am I?"

Well, let's get into it. What's in you, just like anything else that is created, has a blueprint. When we think about the blueprint we must think about the foundation. Your blueprint is the silent guide you carry inside. It is composed of all the things that have shaped you through childhood, your learned attachments, relationships, and experiences. Let's get back to Keischa.

When Keischa was little, she learned that love wasn't unconditional, it had to be earned. She learned and carried this into her adulthood. People "love" her, for sure, but it comes with her participation in the rules. Rules, yup, rules. Rules like: don't be too loud, don't be too needy, don't be what people perceive as "extra", and take only what is given.

She learned that people viewed her as convenient. Keischa also learned to adapt and fit into what everybody expects of her. Their expectations and perceptions have become her reality. Keischa believed that she had given her power away. She realized that she became the helper, the achiever, the peacemaker, and the pleaser. She felt like she was known for being a good person until that narrative did not serve the individual anymore.

The blueprint has shown up in her romantic relationships where she has clearly overplayed her role. She over gave, asked for the least, and got the least. She never expected much and that was the problem. Her expectations were, "I'm not going to get anything in return, so why get excited for anything?"

The blueprint showed up at work. At work she was an over giver, an over pleaser, and a people pleaser. Keischa never wanted to appear difficult, angry, having an attitude, or being a problem because she had always heard that Black women have to be better. You have to be two times better to prove yourself. You couldn't just be yourself because "they" don't expect you to know what you know. She remembered conversations with family where they talked about how, "You have to prove yourself worthy, so they know that you deserve to be where you are."

The blueprint showed up in the spaces where she was alone. Sitting on the couch in tears wondering why nobody saw her, why she felt invisible, why she didn't know where to turn. The struggle. The emptiness. She showed up for everybody else as a loving, empathetic, and empowering person. She poured into everybody: friends, family, coworkers. And then wondered silently why nobody showed up and poured into her.

Keischa's story is our story. We can relate to the struggle of feeling invisible, of feeling lonely, and not knowing what the next step looks like. Running on a hamster wheel that just keeps going and going and going. When we think about our emotional and mental well-being, we often focus on the present, how we feel today, what's overwhelming us, or what we need to do next. But the truth is, our mental health is deeply rooted in something much older, something that has been shaping us since birth: our fundamental needs and the way we form attachments.

OK, so let's talk about that. What shapes the foundation of our needs and mental wellbeing? Listen, don't tune me out just yet, this is actually good. I won't make it too sciency. If that is a word... but you get the point. It's important to our story, the blueprint, to understand how our needs are tied to our actions, thoughts, and behaviors. Let's dive into this foundation and what makes up the blueprint.

Maslow's Hierarchy of Needs is a psychological theory that explains human motivation by prioritizing various human needs in a pyramid structure first explained by the psychologist Abraham Maslow in 1943. It places fundamental needs at the bottom of a pyramid and more open-ended desires at the top with several levels in between.

Maslow's Hierarchy of Needs starts with our basic physical needs with each level developing in nature until we reach the highest version of ourselves. Maslow's theory suggests that we move through five levels of needs:

1. Physiological Needs : Basic survival needs like food, water, and sleep.
2. Safety Needs: A sense of security, stability, and protection.

3. Love and Belonging: Relationships, friendships, and emotional intimacy.

4. Esteem Needs: Self-respect, recognition, and confidence.

5. Self-Actualization: Personal growth, purpose, and fulfillment.

Now, because nothing in this life is explained through a single focus we have an additional layer that builds our foundation. This is where another theory comes into play, Attachment Theory. This theory was originally developed by John Bowlby and focuses on the importance of open intimately emotional relationships. This theory connects what we lacked in childhood with how those unmet needs shape our connection with others and ourselves. The four primary attachment styles are:

1. Secure Attachment: If as a child you felt safe and loved consistently and trusted easily, you probably feel comfortable with intimacy and are generally able to trust others.

2. Anxious Attachment: If as a child love felt unpredictable or absent, your nervous system adapted for survival. You may crave reassurance, but fear abandonment. You may crave closeness, but fear rejection.

3. Avoidant Attachment: If as a child you learned to rely only on yourself because vulnerability felt unsafe, you may struggle with vulnerability and push others away.

4. Disorganized: If as a child you grew up in chaos or trauma, you may swing between wanting love and fearing it. You may experience a mix of anxiety and avoidance due to past trauma.

Think of it this way: Maslow's theory describes what we need, and Attachment Theory explains what happens when we don't get it. If love, belonging, or safety were missing in childhood we carry that emotional gap into adulthood repeating the same patterns in our friendships, relationships, and how we show up for ourselves. Maybe you find yourself in relationships where you give more than you receive, constantly seeking validation. Or perhaps you struggle to trust others and keep people at arm's length, fearing disappointment. These are not just personality quirks; they are survival adaptations shaped by unmet needs.

It sounds simple enough, right? But there are other elements that keep us from reaching the next level. If you are busy putting out fires, you don't have time to think about love or purpose. Survival is about making it to tomorrow. Thriving? That's a luxury you haven't had time to dream about. If you are always stuck at level one, trying to survive, you can't move up to level two, which is feeling secure and safe.

Have you heard or said the phrases: "If it's not one thing it's another." "I keep taking one step forward and two steps back." "I'm just waiting for the other shoe to drop?" "It's always something. I can't win for losing."? Phrases like these are representations of programming and a quiet narrative of lack that keeps being passed down, accepted, and repeated. It gives a sense of normalcy to think that collectively this is how everyone's life is.

As we move through the chapters, we will discuss how each phase of the pyramid works and how we can move through them. Listen, sis, no pressure. We are walking this down, holding hands together. Some things may overlap or seem redundant, but repetition is the foundation of understanding and memory. Get it? Ok, let's go!

Remember we talked about our blueprint; it is built in childhood experiences. If you moved around a lot because there was never enough to pay the rent, or if you didn't have enough food and sometimes went without, it shows up in how you navigate life. Your mental wellbeing will be affected because fear of that experience happening again still exists in your mind today. You can't rest in safety when you aren't able to rest on the knowledge that you can eat this month, that you won't be evicted from your home, or you won't lose your income.

What's Your Attachment Story?

Attachment Quiz: Discover Your Style

Take this short quiz to gain insight into your attachment style. Answer honestly based on your experiences and feelings.

1. When you're upset, how do you typically seek comfort?

A) I reach out to loved ones and feel secure in their support.

B) I crave reassurance but worry about being a burden.

C) I prefer to handle things alone and dislike relying on others.

D) I feel torn—I want support, but also push people away.

2. How do you feel about emotional vulnerability in relationships?

A) I feel safe opening up to those I trust.

B) I worry that being vulnerable will make people leave me.

C) I avoid emotional conversations and keep things at surface-level.

D) I struggle between wanting closeness and fearing it.

3. What best describes your experience with trust?

A) I trust people unless they give me a reason not to.

B) I need constant reassurance to feel secure in relationships.

C) I struggle to trust and prefer independence.

D) I trust inconsistently—I want to, but fear betrayal.

4. How do you respond when someone pulls away or becomes distant?

A) I give them space and trust they'll return.

B) I panic and try to regain their attention.

C) I shut down emotionally and act like I don't care.

D) I feel confused and react in unpredictable ways.

Results

Mostly A's:

Secure Attachment – You feel comfortable with closeness and independence.

Mostly B's: Anxious Attachment – You crave reassurance, but fear abandonment.

Mostly C's: Avoidant Attachment – You value independence and struggle with emotional intimacy.

Mostly D's: Disorganized Attachment – You experience conflicting emotions about connection.

No matter what your result, remember: Attachment styles are not permanent. They are learned patterns, and with awareness and healing, you can develop healthier, more secure relationships.

Let's go deeper. I want you to take a moment and reflect on these questions. Grab a journal or just sit with them for a while. This isn't about judgment; it's about understanding yourself better.

1. Think back to your childhood. How did you know you were loved?

Was love shown through words, actions, or not at all?

Did love feel steady or unpredictable?

2. When you feel emotionally overwhelmed today, what do you do?

Do you reach out?

Shut down?

Overthink?

3. How do you handle conflict in relationships?

Do you avoid it?

Fear it?

Feel comfortable expressing yourself?

4. Do you trust yourself to make good decisions?

Do you often doubt your own feelings and instincts?

Reflection on Results

Your answers to these questions give insight into your attachment style. The way you love, trust, and even doubt yourself is often a reflection of what you learned growing up. But here's the most important part: You are not stuck here! Healing your attachment wounds is possible. Understanding them is the first step.

The next step is learning to recognize the patterns that no longer serve you and replace them with new, healthier ways of connecting. This might look like setting boundaries without guilt, embracing emotional vulnerability, or practicing self-compassion when old wounds resurface. Healing isn't about perfection, it's about progress. One small step at a time.

Maslow's Hierarchy of Needs and Bowlby's Attachment Theory show us that our struggles are not random, they are connected to deep-seated needs. When those needs weren't met in the past, they shaped how we love, trust, and heal today. But here's the good news: we don't have to stay in survival mode. We can learn to meet our own needs, rewire old patterns, and build emotional security from the inside out. As we move through this book, we will explore how to meet these needs with compassion, healing, and self-love.

Chapter Two

Soul Deep: Unpacking the Weight We Carry

"When I dare to be powerful—to use my strength in the service of my vision, then it becomes less and less important whether I am afraid." — Audre Lorde

Growth is a process that doesn't just reach upward, it digs downward too. Remember how we connected our growth to the growth of the tree earlier? This narrative shows that we can only grow tall if our roots are anchored deep. Emotional and psychological well-being depends on nurturing what lies beneath the surface. What we bury doesn't disappear; it shapes us. You know me! We gon' walk this thing down gently because we deal with enough harshness in our lives. Let's begin to uncover the roots of our experiences, the pain, the memories, and the emotions we've buried.

Keischa

Some mornings, Keischa just stares at the ceiling, the phone buzzing as she snoozes it for the third time before finally dragging herself up. "I can't keep doing this," she mutters, brushing her teeth with one hand and scrolling through social media with the other. *"I'm exhausted, bored, and over it. The harder I work, the harder it is to get ahead. What was all that overtime for? No matter how hard I go, it feels like I'm always playing catch-up—rent, bills, groceries, gas, kids and their needs, other people's needs and helping in general. Doing all this at the expense of my own sanity.*

Every morning feels like déjà vu—same alarm, same routine, same numb autopilot. I get up, go to work, and handle everything for everyone. It's crazy because when someone finally texts, "What's up? How are you doing?" I usually text back mindlessly, "I'm fine," even though I'm not and keep pushing through. Shit, what else can I do?

I'm tired. Not just tired like "take a nap" or like everybody keeps saying "get some rest" tired. That advice always gets me. "Get some rest!" What does that mean and how do I do it?! It's soul-deep tired. The kind of tired that lingers no matter how long you sleep. The kind that wraps itself around you and whispers, 'Keep going,' even when you've got nothing left to give."

Lately, in the quiet moments, in the chaos, in the chatter, echoing louder than usual are the questions Keischa asks herself, damn near every hour at this point: "Is this all there is? Why do I do what I do? Why do I hide my real feelings and just push through the pain of doing everything myself?"

As Keischa stared in the bathroom mirror, she thought about her fifteen year old self. Remembering her first real encounter with buried pain. Her Mother had said something during an argument. Well, not really an argument. You know the kind of argument that's one sided? You are just listening to someone yell at you and spill all the stuff they feel like saying. Hurtful stuff that isn't true. But they are adults and can say what they damn well please. Even the kind of things that cut you deep because it comes from someone you love and is supposed to love you. Yeah, that kind of "argument". She couldn't remember her exact words, but she remembered how they felt: sharp, hurtful, demeaning, and unforgiving. She remembered how heavy her body felt. She felt weak, small, and drained as she ran to her room, slammed the door, and collapsed onto her bed sobbing into the pillow.

But even in that moment of raw emotion, she willed herself to stop. *Don't cry too long. Don't let her see.* She remembered how she felt like she had gained a superpower as she clenched her fists and let the tears dry on their own. That night, she made a quiet decision, a vow: tuck the pain away, deep inside, and pretend it doesn't matter. Because in that moment, at that time, it didn't.

Later that day, Keischa sat in her mothers driveway, waiting to pick the kids up. Thank God, her mom had picked them up from school, the boss had called a mandatory meeting that could have been an email, it was exhausting working there. She sat in silence thinking how her mom had done all this. She thought about how she was always so proud to hear people say her mom was a strong woman. How had she gotten this title?? Keischa was in deep thought. What had she missed? How was it that she always felt like she was drowning or like a failure, but kept going? How did she keep showing up for her kids, but inside wanted to lie under the covers and sleep? She was being intentional to not cry in front of her children. She never wanted to show weakness and she wanted them to see her as strong too. She worked two jobs. She didn't rest. She coped. She learned that silence is safer than expressing your need. You learn that love sometimes looks like absence, because, "I got to work to take care of you," which leads to the belief that finances are more important than connection, and that safety means self-reliance.

The Roots

At fifteen, Keischa's first root was buried. Like so many of us, Keischa believed that by burying it she had control over it. But roots don't stop growing just because we refuse to look at them. By the time she hit her mid-twenties, that root had twisted its way into other parts of life blooming as anxiety, self-doubt, and a sense of isolation she couldn't seem to shake.

This is the nature of unresolved pain: it doesn't stay neatly tucked away. It seeps out in our interactions with others, in the way we talk to ourselves, and in the walls we build between us and the love we crave. When our attachment needs are left unmet or wounded, it complicates everything. Suddenly, relationships feel risky, vulnerability feels dangerous, and self-love feels impossible.

Healing isn't about undoing the past, but about integrating it by giving pain a voice instead of suffering in silence. You won't erase anger, grief, and disappointment, but you will gain the realization that healing means that it's ok to validate and hold space for those feelings, letting them exist without allowing them to be your definition of yourself.

People and situations sometimes make it hard to find safety, to be open or vulnerable, and to say things you would never say out loud. Hearing recurring comments, being in similar situations, and having different people reinforce negative labels like; "too sensitive," "too much," or "not enough" slowly begins to make you believe these false perceptions instead of the truths you knew about yourself. Pain becomes buried and swallowed as you accept what others give and define as who you are. These learned behaviors and false truths dictate what you need. What you missed as a child and what you deserve now becomes less important and loud. You believe the irrational thoughts because if enough people say something about you, it feels true. You begin trying to fix something you didn't break yet are quite sure is broken.

It isn't just the pain of a harsh word or a bad breakup. It's the absence of softness. The absence of reassurance. The longing for someone to say, "I see you. You matter. You're safe here." When you grow up emotionally hungry, you learn to ration your needs, to stop asking for too much, and eventually, to stop asking altogether. But silence doesn't protect us, it isolates us.

I share this because I know what it's like to feel crushed under the weight of unmet needs, unresolved memories, and buried roots. But I also know the freedom that comes when you begin to dig and give yourself permission to acknowledge what you've buried to learn from it.

Healing is a process, and every root you uncover brings you closer to understanding yourself. Don't rush it. Be gentle with yourself. Remember, the deeper the roots, the stronger the tree. This is the story so many of us know. We were raised to survive, not to thrive. We learned to be strong, to push through, to keep going. We learned patterns that helped us cope, but now those same patterns are keeping us stuck. Those patterns, routines, and cycles feel safe because they're familiar, but silently suffocate us. It's a struggle to move beyond the known, especially when we were never taught how to do so.

Keischa's story is not just hers, it's ours. It's the collective fatigue of Black women raised on resilience. It's the internalized belief that being tired is just the price we pay to keep things together. But what if keeping it all together is what's keeping us from healing?

Here's what no one tells you: those learned behaviors become emotional routines. Just like brushing your teeth or locking the door, our bodies and minds return to those coping habits automatically. Maslow's theory reminds us that we can't move up the pyramid toward love, esteem, and self-actualization if our safety needs remain tangled in trauma or if our beliefs about love are rooted in fear. Attachment theory reminds us that how we bond is how we survive. But when survival is all we know, thriving feels foreign.

This is the hamster wheel we sometimes feel stuck on. Not because of weakness or because we don't want more, but because we are functioning on outdated information. And let's be real, when you've been taught that breaking the routine means risking everything, staying put starts to feel like the safest bet. So how do we step off the wheel? Well, first, we notice we're on it.

Mental Health Exercise: Root Mapping

This exercise is about identifying the emotional roots tied to your attachment experiences—whether from childhood, relationships, or recent events—and understanding their role in your current emotional landscape.

1. Create a calm environment.

Find a quiet space where you feel safe. Set the mood with soft lighting or calming music if it helps.

2. Draw your tree.

On a sheet of paper, sketch a simple tree. The trunk represents you, standing tall.

3. Label your roots.

Think about three experiences that shaped how you attach or connect to others. These might be childhood memories, relationships, or pivotal moments when your needs for love, safety, or validation were met—or left unmet. Label each experience along a different root.

4. Write it out.

Next to each root, write a few sentences about the emotions tied to that experience. Were you hurt? Did you feel abandoned, unseen, or misunderstood? Be honest and compassionate.

5. Identify growth opportunities.

For each root, reflect on how that experience influences you today. Does it cause you to pull back from relationships or seek reassurance? Write one small way you can nurture growth from this root, such as setting a boundary, expressing your needs, or practicing self-compassion.

6. Ground yourself with affirmations or a prayer.

- I am worthy of love and connection.
- My past does not define my future.
- I am growing stronger every day.

Strategy: Recognizing Emotional Routines

Before we change anything, we need to notice what we're doing. Answer the questions honestly. Grab your journal or a piece of paper.

Self-Assessment: Are You Stuck in Survival Mode?

1.   Do you often feel emotionally drained even after a full night's sleep?

2.   Do you struggle to ask for help or feel guilty when you do?

3.   Do you repeat the same types of relationships, even if they're unfulfilling or harmful?

4.   Are you more comfortable giving love than receiving it?

5.   Do you feel anxious or unsafe when things are calm or going well?

If you answered "yes" to three or more, your emotional routine might be stuck in survival mode. This awareness is not a verdict—it's a beginning.

Coping Strategy: The Pause + Pattern Journal

When you're stuck in a loop, the most powerful thing you can do is pause.

Here's how to practice it:

1.   Pause Daily.

At the end of each day, take five minutes to reflect. Ask yourself: What did I feel most today? When did I feel most like myself?

2.   Name the Pattern.

Was there a moment you shut down instead of speaking up? Did you say "yes" when you meant "no"? These are your emotional routines.

3.   Explore the Root.

What experience does that behavior connect to? Is it rooted in fear of rejection, abandonment, or the need to control?

4.   Reframe with Compassion

Write one sentence to reframe the belief. For example, instead of, "If I ask for help, I'm weak," try, "Asking for help is a strength and a right."

Repeat this exercise for 21 days and see what you learn. Awareness is the doorway to change.

Affirmations for Rewiring Your Roots

Speak these aloud or write them in your journal.

- I am allowed to rest. I do not have to earn peace.
- I am not a burden for needing care.
- I am learning new ways to love and be loved.
- My routines can reflect who I am becoming, not just who I've been.

- I trust myself to grow beyond what I was taught.

Healing is not just about what we do, it's about what we unlearn. It's about rewriting the blueprint, one pattern at a time. It's about choosing to pause. You're not broken. You're blooming. And this time, you're blooming on purpose.

Reflection Questions for Discussion or Journaling

1. What emotional routine do you find yourself repeating, even when it no longer serves you?
2. Where did you learn that being strong meant being silent?
3. How does your body respond when you're emotionally overwhelmed?
4. Who in your life modeled emotional survival for you—and what do you want to keep or release from their example?
5. What is one belief about love, rest, or help that you're ready to unlearn?
6. If you could rewrite your emotional blueprint, what's one new pattern you'd like to create?
7. What would it feel like to give yourself permission to rest, ask for help, or say no?
8. How can you create more space in your life for emotional safety and self-trust?

Scripture for Reflection

"The Lord is close to the brokenhearted and saves those who are crushed in spirit." — Psalm 34:18

"Do not conform to the pattern of this world but be transformed by the renewing of your mind." — Romans 12:2

Love Note

Remember this: the routines you've relied on were survival strategies. But you are allowed to outgrow survival. You are allowed to evolve. You're not behind. You're just beginning.

Chapter Three

Safety Ain't Optional

"You can't heal in the same place you got sick. Choose peace — even if it means starting over." — Unknown

Often, we rely on the familiar to get us through the pain of not feeling safe or secure. We walk through life focusing on making it through the day, so that we can function. We go back to old narratives and scenarios that allow us to regain, or believe, the illusion of safety. When we don't know what to do, we rely on what we have in our purse, in our background, and what we know worked before.

Keischa

In the evening, Keischa stood in her bedroom staring at the closet as the memory of her six year old self flooded her senses. She remembers hiding in a closet during one of her parents' loud arguments. Her heart pounded as she pressed her knees to her chest. That moment etched itself into her nervous system. She learned that silence was safer than asking for comfort and that stillness might protect her from the next emotional eruption.

Keischa didn't just wake up one day feeling unsafe. She was raised in a home where safety was unpredictable. Her childhood was filled with episodes that left her feeling like she was walking on eggshells. You know what that's like. It's very much like being on a teeter totter. Truth be told, she never liked that up and down feeling. The sense of having no control bothered her. It was off-putting that the other party could just decide to get off, with or without, warning.

The part of her childhood she hated most was never quite knowing what would piss her mom off. She never knew if answering or asking a question jokily today, like she did yesterday, would result in laughter or a full blown rant about disrespect. Yeah, she knew the feeling of walking on eggshells way too well. Her father was an alcoholic. He could go from days of being almost invisible, to one day being loud, toxic, and embarrassing as hell. Yikes, talk about unpredictably.

Her mother was emotionally unavailable, battling her own depression and struggles. There was no room for Keischa to cry, question, or need. She learned early that vulnerability could be dangerous. Her childhood consisted of not feeling safe. Having somewhere to live wasn't the issue, but "home" was an unfamiliar term. She never felt like she had what others described to her as a home. Somehow everything, including housing, always felt temporary.

Keischa could never settle in. She constantly tried to be quiet and small so that she would not upset anyone and have to leave to find something to do outside of the house. This continued into adulthood when she shared a living space with a roommate. Keisha tried to be as nice as possible. She gave people what they needed, what they wanted to be accepted. She never wanted to be seen as a burden, so she always paid her share, made herself useful, gleefully pitching in. She always made sure she didn't rock the boat. Even with all this effort she felt uneasy, unsettled, and unwanted.

She was never sure how to feel, how to fit in, and how to be... herself. She feared being seen. She feared not being seen. She learned to escape by being smart and not causing trouble. "Being a good girl." Little Keischa grew up. But guess what? So did her unhealed wounds.

See, when you grow up in chaos you don't ask for peace, you build survival habits. You become the peacekeeper. The protector. The fixer. The one who anticipates tension and softens it with your own silence. It's ironic, because Keischa never felt anyone held those roles for her. Nobody came to her rescue to fulfill those missing pieces.

She became the "strong friend." The dependable one. She got good grades, kept the peace, and tried not to make waves. Keischa used to think being "strong" meant keeping it all in, but this kind of strength is a reaction to fear. She didn't want to get hurt. What showed up on the outside definitely did not mirror her inside emotions. On the inside, she was still trying to fit in, find her place, be validated, and feel worthy.

The journey to adulthood brings different challenges than childhood, but we will manage them the same if we haven't learned the tools to heal. Keischa doesn't know how to change. She wasn't taught to heal and is still doing the same performance, the same dance, to get safety and security – the things she really desires.

She understood that her insecurities could be used as weapons against her by so-called "friends and loved ones." She began rehearsing conversations in her head, before speaking out loud. She began to protect herself using humor, sarcasm, and what others deemed as meanness to form a bubble of protection. When you feel unsafe in your environment, you begin checking your tone, your volume, and your face. When you don't have emotional safety, you feel like you get punished for being you. You understand that being in your truth can be used against you.

For Keischa, unwanted memories and feelings often showed up. There was constant pressure to make sure people were comfortable with her. It had been ingrained in her that it was improper not to be on, not to be smiley. She learned not to be human, but a thing that could be tolerated. Still, people complained about her expressions. Wow, imagine that! People really out here mad about how you hold your own face saying things like, "Girl, what's wrong with you? Fix your face. Why you mad? Smile!" as if she were a clown there for entertainment.

Which is wild, because none of that is a thing! That is just how she held her face. Because of the judgement, Keischa always did a face check in meetings, social situations, and in important rooms so that the perception of her character wasn't negative. It's hard to understand how people judge when you are simply displaying your own face. A lot of anxiety comes from knowing you're not just living, you're managing perceptions, calculating risk, and trying to keep safe.

People criticized Keischa's goals, thoughts, appearance, and made slick comments all in the name of "keeping it real." When she reacted they would say, "Girl, you being too sensitive," and the most famous, "I'm just joking."

They'd say stuff like:
"You so bougie?" (ha, ha)

"Oh OK, I see you. Must be nice."

"Why you always so sarcastic?"

"You back in school?"

"You gaining weight?"

"Ain't you supposed to be…[insert whatever title they were demeaning at the time]."

Patterns

As we reflect on wounds, pains, and hurts we can see things from our past that follow patterns. Pain resurfaces over and over in the way we are still treated. We use what we were taught and past behaviors to perform so that we can cover up to feel safe.

We were taught to ignore pain. Somebody being mean to us? Ignore them. Somebody being toxic to you? Remember the old rhyme: Sticks and stones may break my bones, but words will never hurt me.

Well, we knew then and know now: that is bullshit!! Words definitely have the capacity to hurt. We are taught a myriad of things like:

Smile even though you're hurting inside. Laugh it off.

Be grateful! Some people have it worse.

Be quiet.

Be agreeable.

But, sis, that's not safety, that's the underlay for the overplay. That's pushing everything down inside of you and destroying your nervous system. In fact, that's submission. Understanding your wounds and need for safety and security means creating a space where your nervous system can exhale. It's hard to create this space when safety has been inconsistent or denied. Or when your nervous system never settled. You stay alert, anxious, and exhausted. When you begin to learn how to create and embrace a safe inner space, it makes it easier for your "no" to be a complete sentence, for your response not to be overexplained, and your softness not mistaken for weakness.

We as Black women have been praised for how much we can carry. We have accepted this narrative as if it were a badge to be displayed. A label to be honored. But let me say this with love. Just because you can survive the fire doesn't mean you should keep walking through the flames. We are not here to suffer gracefully. We are not here to normalize the absence of peace. You deserve to feel safe. Period!

We are not talking about safety as in putting locks and alarms on your home and car. It's more about the safety we can't buy with an insurance policy. It's the kind of safety that satisfies the need to be safe in your body, in your spirit, and in your mind. The kind of safety where your body unclenches, your shoulders relax, and your body settles. That feeling of working all day, coming home, taking off your bra and flopping on the comfortable couch. The amazing feeling where your mind is safe to let go of that never ending to-do list, the release of thinking you need to fix everyone's problems, and space for your thoughts to stop racing. That moment of security when you don't have to scan the room or rehearse your responses. And gurllll, here's the real tea, the real real: it's the space where you're not shrinking yourself to stay or to be liked. Bayyybee, that kind of safety is chefs' kiss.

Emotional Safety: The Soft Place You've Always Needed

Emotional safety is knowing your truth won't be used against you, understanding that your feelings hold weight, and whether or not others agree, they still are honored and validated. It's having relationships where you don't need a mask or a filter. You feel safe in being emotional, vulnerable, and yes, even messy without being told to shut up, calm down, or being shut out. It's the moment your nervous system sighs and says, *"I'm safe here, I can let my guard down."*

If you've been living in fight-or-flight mode– when your body's physiological instinct to respond to a threat either prepares you to physically protect yourself or you take flight (getting yourself up outta there), safety might feel foreign. You might confuse chaos with connection. You might think "guarded" is your personality. You might even call your hyper-independence "strength." Black women often carry the unspoken burden of hypervigilance. The Strong Black Woman persona. This narrative doesn't leave room for vulnerability or humanness, let alone emotional safety.

Let me tell you something. It's not strength if it's built on fear, on other people's perception of what you need, or what your strength "should" look like. Safety sits at the very foundation of Maslow's Hierarchy of Needs. You remember the pyramid we talked about? That triangle of basic human motivation? Before we can chase dreams, build community, or become our highest self, we need to feel safe.

Not just physically, but emotionally, psychologically, and relationally. As we move up the pyramid, we see that the second level of Maslow's hierarchy is the Need for Safety and Security. It includes more than just protection from physical harm. It covers:

Emotional security: feeling free from emotional abuse and relational chaos.

Financial stability: knowing your basic needs will be met without constant fear of lack.

Health security: being able to care for your body and access healthcare without barriers.

Order and structure: having routines, predictable environments, and a sense of control over your life.

Law and protection: trusting that systems, communities, and even your own home won't turn against you.

Emotional safety means you don't have to brace yourself all the damn time. It means you can say, "I'm not okay", without feeling like you're too much. It means that you are not always living in a space of "what's next?" Or constantly living with so much anxiety that you don't have the luxury to even believe things can be better. It means you can show up messy, honest, real, and still be loved.

It looks like:

Having space to speak and be heard. Really heard.

Feeling protected, not picked apart.

Knowing you're allowed to just be. No mask, no hustle, no proving.

What's Actually Happening in Your Brain and Body?

If you've spent years waiting for the other shoe to drop, there is no such thing as rest. Your amygdala is your brain's built-in alarm system. It's designed to protect you by detecting threats. If you've lived through trauma, childhood neglect, emotional abandonment, emotional volatility, or just chronic stress, that alarm gets hypervigilant. Your brain wires itself for survival, not joy. It's like a smoke detector going off every time you make toast. You normalize it and it begins to be familiar. In the same way, over time, your system starts to adapt to the situation.

Your prefrontal cortex, the rational part of your brain, tries to calm the system down. But when the amygdala is constantly shouting "DANGER!" it can override logic and reality.

When your brain perceives danger, it sends signals to your body to prepare for threat:

Your heart races — pumping blood to your limbs so you can run or fight.

Your muscles tighten — ready for defense.

Your digestion slows — because your body isn't worried about lunch when it thinks you might not survive the next five minutes.

Your breathing becomes shallow — to conserve energy and stay alert.

Your cortisol spikes — flooding your bloodstream with stress hormones.

Here's the kicker; when any part of the step of the pyramid is missing — your body can begin to normalize chronic stress. Stress becomes your default setting. You start to work within that "normal" to make things make sense when they do not. Imagine, there is a broken step on our porch. You adapt to that step missing. It becomes automatic to avoid the danger. In the same way, your body is trying its best to avoid danger. Even when the danger is gone.

It is also why:

You feel exhausted even after sleeping.

You can't trust a good moment because you are always waiting for the other shoe to drop.

You numb out to survive your day by being on autopilot.

You start sabotaging peace because your body doesn't recognize it yet.

Here's the powerful part: You can teach your body a new truth. You can unlearn old narratives and replace them with new thoughts, strategies, and skills. Your brain can learn that not everything is a threat. Your body can learn what peace feels like. Your soul can finally exhale.

While this book is meant to be a page turner it is definitely about self-care, self-love, and self-awareness. So, let's slow it down a bit, close our collective eyes, and breathe. Put your hand on your heart, close your eyes, breathe in deeply, and out deeply. Repeat three times and relax. Slowly open your eyes.

Maslow's Hierarchy Revisited

Can you believe that we are only three chapters in? We've peeled back layers, some raw, some tender, some we didn't even realize were still buried underneath the surface, all while getting close to our homegirl, Keischa.

This book is intended to be a mirror, a permission slip, and a new path. As we climb to the next level of the pyramid, remember we are getting back to the version of you that isn't blindsided by the noise, performance, roles, titles, or trauma. Let's do a review and remember we are securing the bag, moving up the pyramid to our best version of self, and how attachment plays a role in how we love and place value on relationships.

You remember Maslow? We talked about him earlier in the chapters. He built this theory designed as a pyramid to reflect what every human needs to feel whole. As we go through the steps, we are reminded of the truth that human needs are more than basic food and shelter. And that the Black woman's climb to feeling whole has always been steeper. Our climb is not linear. It's layered.

It includes needing safety and support against generational trauma, as Black women have to manage higher levels of stress and related illness. Safety is complicated, it includes safety from racialized stereotypes (angry, aggressive, incompetent) and microaggressions.

Love and Belonging for Black women often requires performing several roles at one time without the needed or wanted support.. As we work with the foundation of Maslow's Theory we are reminded that the pyramid assumes that once a need is met, it no longer requires attention. But for Black women, needs recycle. Safety must be renegotiated. Belonging must be protected. So for us, the climb is not only upward, it is constant.

Our physiological needs are warped as we are conditioned to care for others before ourselves. Our feeling of safety is never settled when we build safety around trauma, leaving us consistently searching for backup plans. And our love and belonging? Weeeell, many of us were taught to earn love. The more we showed up and gave perceived value to our audience the more we experienced love.

Attachment Theory Revisited

Our early attachment experiences shape our pyramid. Attachment styles are the love maps we built in childhood. They tell us what to expect from relationships. They speak loudly of whether we trust love to stay or if we have a hustle mentality fixated on how to keep it.

If growing up you were not being celebrated just for existing, you had feelings of being easily dismissed, or if you had to be "good," "quiet," "strong," or "useful" to feel wanted, then baby, it makes sense why you second-guess yourself. The attachment wound is why you over-deliver, over-apologize, and over extend yourself in relationships. This is why you feel like if you stop performing, they might disappear. This is an anxious attachment in action. And it's not your fault. This is your little girl still asking, "Am I enough?"

Your Emotional Safety Routine

Let's make this part of your life, not just a chapter in this book. Make this a habit.

Daily Safety Routine:

1. Morning Mirror Talk:

Say this: *I deserve to feel safe in my body, my mind, and my relationships.*

2. Boundary Check-In:

Ask: *Where am I shrinking today just to keep the peace?*

Then stop shrinking.

3. Nervous System Reset:

- 3 slow breaths with your hand on your chest.
- One song that reminds you who TF you are.
- Step outside for 3 minutes of stillness.

4. Evening Real Talk Journal:

Reflect:

- When did I feel safest today?
- What drained me?
- What do I want more of tomorrow?

Where Do You Feel Safe?

Journal Prompts:

- What does safety feel like in my body?
- Who makes me feel safe, and why?
- Where do I still shrink myself to stay "loved"?

Safety Self-Check (Be Real, No Shame):

- I can cry without apologizing.
- I don't feel guilty when I rest.
- I don't perform in my closest relationships.
- I trust my own feelings.
- I can name two places where I feel emotionally safe.

This is where the work starts. That's where the healing begins. Choose your peace! Let's not just read this chapter. Let's live it.

Self-Talk is essential to your growth, learn to talk to YOU nicely. Say this to yourself out loud:

I am no longer abandoning myself to feel accepted. My safety is sacred.

I am born to thrive in safety.

I heal in softness.

I flourish in wholeness.

Clear something today.

Unfollow the page that triggers you.

Mute the group chat that drains you.

Reschedule the lunch you were dreading.

Peace is not passive. It's a bold choice. And from now on — it's your standard.

Love Note

Phew. Ok, y'all, we've been through a lot and I see you are still here (insert noise makers, confetti, and me smiling from ear to ear)! Ok, enough about me, but yea I'm still cheesin'.

Final Word, sis: Safety ain't a luxury. It's your requirement.

Chapter Four

Worthy Without the Applause: Reclaiming Esteem from the Inside Out

"I am not afraid of storms, for I am learning how to sail my ship."
— Mary Church Terrell, educator and activist

For Black women, esteem has rarely been freely given. Black women typically have to prove our worth in environments that constantly question it. Esteem must be rebuilt after micro-injuries. We have often had to fight for it in corporate boardrooms, beauty aisles, relationships, and even in our own mirrors. We've been taught to shrink, to serve quietly, to not take up too much space. It doesn't just come from the outside, but starts with the inner circle of our family, our "tribe", and people in our life who matter. Or mattered. Esteem can get stuck when you are in survival mode, feeling afraid of saying or doing the wrong thing, constantly being aware of yourself, and watching that you don't show up and out too much. Making sure you fit in so as to not feel the jabs thinly veiled in jokes that you are being "too sensitive", "too emotional", or "too loud." And we're not here to survive anymore. We're here to soar.

And now...settle in y'all and let's get into it. We've arrived here, esteem. Esteem isn't just about confidence. Esteem is not just how others see us, but how we see ourselves through the lens of others and the ways that manifests in how we see ourselves. This is the turning point in our healing. Not toward perfection. But toward peace.

Keischa

"Damn, why do I keep putting myself in this dumb ass space?" Keischa muttered to herself. "Cooking and waiting for someone who I know doesn't care or value me. People keep saying, 'Know your worth.' How? And what does that even mean? I know it, but how do I get others to? Startled out of her thoughts, she reached for her cell phone when it buzzed then rang loud as hell. *Why do I have the ringer that loud?* Keischa thought as she quickly answered.

"What up, where you? You said you were coming through hours ago," Keischa spoke to her man, Malcolm.

His response, same as always, "Here you go. I'll be through tonight. With your thick ass," and then hanging up.

Keischa knew what that meant: sex. She felt disrespected, but did not say anything. She felt sick because she knew he was calling her fat with that thick comment. Routinely, right on cue, she began clearing the dishes. Next, putting away the food, blowing out the candles, heading to the couch with a bottle of wine, a blanket, and tears to keep her company. In her mind this was routine and disappointing. She wasn't disappointed in him, but in herself. "Why are you so freaking desperate?" she kept saying in a whisper as she sipped her wine.

Sitting on the couch, finishing off the bottle of wine, Keischa was transported to a memory of her eight year old self. She was standing in the doorway, watching her mom twist in the mirror, tugging at her blouse, sighing with disappointment.

"Ugh, I need to stop eating bread," her mother sighed, not to anyone in particular, turning sideways to assess her stomach. Keischa shyly asked her mom what was wrong. She remembered her sharp tone, and look of disgust saying, "I'm so fat". Keischa just stood there staring at her confused. She didn't know anything about the concept of being fat. What was fat? She did not know what it meant, but her mothers words and actions made it clear it was something she did not want to be.

The memory flooded her thoughts as tears rolled uncontrollably. She recalled what happened next. That night, she made the decision to trade what she wanted with what she thought was a better option. Keischa pushed her cornbread to the edge of her plate. Looking back, it was weird that no one noticed. Everyone knew she loved bread. Especially the hot out the oven honey and real butter cornbread.

By thirteen, Keischa had learned to suck in her belly when she laughed, to pull at her shirt when she sat down, and to keep her jacket on. Not because she hated herself, but she learned that's what women did. They shrunk, fit in, and made sure they were "presentable." Her mother rarely offered compliments or emotional comfort. In fact, it was quite the opposite. Her mother would scold, "Don't have seconds, you gon' have to shop in the husky section." Unintentionally, Keischa's hand immediately landed on her stomach in disgust as the memory lingered.

But, Keischa remembered that as her weight increased the praise of being smart did also. She would be praised for achievements: good grades, clean rooms, being helpful, and being quiet. But there was no reward for feelings. No softness. No compassion for Keischa's tears after being teased at school for her size. She learned early to be good, be helpful, excel in academics, and don't take up too much space. Above all, don't ask for too much.

That's how she ended up here on the couch alone in tears, wanting. Wanting to be loved, chosen. Grown Keischa was still performing, just with higher stakes and prettier masks. Still hoping that if she can be good enough, helpful enough, low maintenance enough, that "they" won't leave.

She gave to relationships until she was empty. Dated these men who didn't know how to hold her, protect her, or see her. But she stayed. Because something still whispered, *"If I leave, I'll be nothing. If I speak up, I'll be too much."* Imagine cooking meals to keep a man who isn't feeding you emotionally.

Her performance wasn't limited to romantic relationships. She became the friend who stayed up all night talking others through their heartbreaks, but had no space to cry for her own. She wore achievement like armor. People would clap for her, out of obligation, but no one really saw her.

In her twenties, Keischa remembered that she made herself useful to every man she dated. Cooked like a wife. Showed up like a therapist. Loved like her survival depended on it. Because in some ways, it did. She didn't know love could be safe. How could she have? She hadn't seen it.

She began to confuse being needed with being wanted, and confused control with care. This behavior was often reinforced by friends who knew the same kind of love. They had the same cultural beliefs and coping patterns. The repeated narratives of family or friends can be unhealthy and they taught Keischa if she could just be better, mold herself into what they needed, and play small she would be chosen. This led to many nights of being unsatisfied and staying too long in toxic and unhealthy spaces.

She began to realize that she said "yes" far too many times when her body was begging her to say "NO!!" She bought birthday gifts, took trips, and loaned money (that was never returned) to friends who didn't reciprocate. Keischa held space for everybody and cried alone in her car, because no one was holding space for her. She was consistently available for everyone, except herself.

She looked like she had it all together on the outside, but behind closed doors she cried silently into her pillow while scrolling Instagram, wondering why love always seemed to cost her more than it gave. The pain of pretending would hit her sometimes as she told herself, *"I'm just loyal."* The painful, gnawing, knowing deep down told her she was scared. Yup, scared that if she stopped giving, the people she loved would stop choosing her. Without her usefulness, she wasn't worth keeping around.

And the worst part? Keischa had learned her role so well that she felt like people no longer saw her as human, but as a means to an end. She was the one who had learned to make pain look polite. Learned to cloak herself in "strength" and pretend to be well. She dressed up her emptiness. She wore her consistent, almost robotic, response of, "I'm good", like a costume. But beneath it all was a little girl still trying to earn her place in the world. Still thinking love had to be negotiated. Still thinking, *"If I give enough, maybe someone will finally choose me for real."* Tonight when Keischa stood broken in her kitchen, barefoot, clutching her robe, staring at the leftovers (Can you call food that nobody ate leftovers?) she had felt stupid.

She was stupid to fall for the same trap again. Showing up for a man who never showed up for her. Her phone was dry. Her energy was gone. Her heart? Heavy. The silence in the room wasn't peaceful. It was loud. It echoed. She sat at the edge of her couch, holding the cell phone tightly. Willing it to ring, she prayed for his text like that would validate that she meant something to him. Like it was proof that she was willing to give her all to the relationship, to try again. "Again", she said out loud And that's when it happened. Not a breakdown, just a quiet question in her chest: *"Is this all there is?"*

The question sat heavy. Because she knew it wasn't just about the man. It was about all the ways she'd been stretching herself thin just to feel seen. The ways she had betrayed her heart, her emotions, and her needs. Forgetting at times what her needs actually were. Remembering every time she said "yes" because she was too afraid "no" would leave her alone. All the ways she made herself smaller just to be picked, just to be part of the tribe.

In that moment, alone, tired, she realized something: she'd spent her whole life choosing others. And she had no idea how to choose herself. She just sat there, holding the ache. Holding the truth. Because somewhere deep inside, something was shifting.It wasn't loud. It wasn't dramatic. But it was real.

The performance was cracking. And through the cracks, through the tears, through the lump making it hard to swallow, her real self, the one she buried to be accepted, was whispering: *"I miss you,girl. Where did you go?"*

She walked to the bathroom, the only place in the house where she ever let herself fall apart. She didn't look in the mirror. Instead, she turned on the shower and sat on the closed toilet lid and folded into herself. Arms wrapped tight like she was holding a baby, her chest rose and fell with short, uneven breaths. Not quite crying. Not quite numb. Just... unraveling.

Her phone buzzed. It was a text from a cousin asking for help. Well, not really asking. It was more like helping herself to Keischa's time, peace, and solitude by wanting her help moving this weekend. Another request without even a "hello" or a thought that she might be busy, or not want to move no damn furniture for the second time this year. Another moment where she was expected to show up without question. She stared at the screen. "Ughh," she groaned, and yet at the same time the familiar urge rushed her to say yes. To be there. Be needed. But something in her paused. Something deep in her belly whispered, *"What about you?"*

It startled her. She hadn't thought about her own needs in so long, let alone voice them. She didn't even recognize the voice. It sounded like a stranger's voice. She slowly turned the phone over and placed it screen-down on the sink. Keischa wasn't ready to say no, not yet. But she wasn't ready to keep saying yes either. And for the first time, that didn't feel selfish. It felt like the beginning of loving, starting with liking, herself.

It was a small return to the little girl who used to laugh with her whole body. The one who wore mismatched socks and asked too many questions. Who read books that took her everywhere. The little girl that dreamed big dreams and loved television.The one who somehow got lost at eight years old and slid her cornbread off her plate. She forgot it was possible to be loved just because she existed. That little girl still lived in her. Not broken. Just buried. And tonight, in the quiet of her own bathroom, Keischa felt her stir.

Tools to Reclaim Your Esteem

Sis, now that we walked Keischa's story down, let's talk about how you can start moving from performance-based worth to rooted self-love and elevated self-esteem. Let's start the ground work on the true you, making your self-esteem a reflection of who you are. Remember, we are moving up the pyramid to your best self. This isn't about overnight miracles or perfection. It's about small moments of choice. Moments of reflection and spaces where you choose you just a little differently. Let's get into it.

1. The "I Am Enough" Mirror Moment

This might feel weird at first, but grab a mirror and look yourself right in the eyes. No distractions, no makeup filters, no judgment. Say aloud: *"I am enough. I am worthy just as I am."*

If it feels shaky, try this: smile while you say it. It tricks your brain into believing it a little more each time. Do this daily, even if you don't believe it yet.

Why it works: You're literally rewiring your brain to shift from "I have to prove myself" to "I exist, therefore I am worthy."

2. The "Stop Shrinking" Challenge

For one whole day, try this:

- Notice every time you catch yourself minimizing your needs or silencing your feelings.

- When you notice, pause and ask yourself: *"What would it look like if I took up this space instead?"*

- Practice saying one small boundary or honest feeling out loud, even if it's just to yourself.

Examples:

"I need a break."

"I don't want to do that."

"I'm feeling overwhelmed."

This is not about being rude or shutting people out — it's about honoring your real self.

Why it works: It starts to build your muscle of self-respect and lets your true voice breathe.

3. The "Good Enough" Gratitude Jar

Get a jar or a container and every day write down one thing you did that was good enough — not perfect, not extra — just good enough.

Examples:

- Took a nap when tired.
- Said no without guilt.
- Cooked a simple meal.
- Asked for help.
- Took five deep breaths when stressed.

Put these notes in the jar. When you're feeling low, open the jar and read your own proof of worth.

Why it works: It rewires your focus from "I'm not enough" to "Look at how I'm showing up, even in small ways."

4. The "Love Letter to Little You"

Write a letter to your inner child — that little girl who had to shrink to survive.

Tell her:

- She is loved beyond measure.
- She didn't deserve to have to shrink.
- Her worth was never dependent on performance.
- She is seen and held now.

Read this letter whenever you feel small or unworthy. You can even read it aloud in your safe space.

Why it works: This heals attachment wounds by offering the love and validation little you didn't get.

5. The "Permission Slip" Ritual

Create your own permission slip — a written or spoken statement giving yourself the right to:

- Take up space.
- Say no.
- Rest without guilt.

- Ask for what you need.
- Be imperfect.

Keep it somewhere visible — your bathroom mirror, your phone notes, your planner. Say it to yourself whenever you feel doubt creeping in.

Why it works: Giving yourself explicit permission dismantles the unconscious scripts of shrinkage.

Love Note

Your worth isn't tied to what you do, how much you give, or how perfectly you perform. Your worth is who you are. Take time to remember your little self and use these experiences to learn your older YOU. It's okay to feel scared when you start showing up for yourself differently. That's part of growth. But I promise you are worth every step of this climb.

Chapter Five

Love and Belonging: The Ache for Love

"I found God in myself, and I loved her. I loved her fiercely."
– Ntozake Shange

Keischa

You ever just... felt like... "blah"? No explanation for it, no rhyme or reason. Just "blah" like the color grey. Nothing felt good, and the crazy thing was, nothing felt particularly bad. This Wednesday felt like a weighted blanket, but not in a good cozy secure way. It kinda hung there like a coat you couldn't take off.

Keischa thought to herself, *"Damn, this day seems sooo long."* Sitting in her car after her lunch break felt comfortable, safe. It felt like solitude. Until she realized she was parked a little too long outside her job. *"I can't be late again,"* she thought and quickly clutched her sandwich in her hand. She made it earlier to save money, but hadn't taken a bite of it. *"Why do I keep 'making' lunch knowing I'm not going to eat it?! It defeats the purpose of supposedly saving money."*

Her thoughts were interrupted by the phone buzzing with a text from Malcom: *"You good?"* She stared at it. That simple question could mean anything, but for Keischa, it was heavy. It was loaded. And it never quite felt like caring. It felt like checking in just enough to say you checked in, but not enough to care. The man she was dating wasn't cruel, but he wasn't consistent. It had been almost two weeks since he had ditched her dinner. No calls, no nothing. Now out of nowhere, a text. Now what? There was something familiar about this situation, about him, though. Keischa couldn't quite put her finger on it.

A song started playing from her playlist that brought up a memory of being eleven years old watching her mother listening to music in the living room. Not in a joyful fun way that she had heard people talk about. They talked about waking up on a Saturday morning, windows open with a light breeze and sunlight streaming in. Anita Baker would be blaring loudly signaling it was time to get up and get to cleaning. No, this wasn't that. It was more of a sadness, a longing. Waiting for a man who never came. Keischa learned early that she did not want that. The music was playing, but in the stillness it felt silent. That moment taught her not to wait on anyone. Not to need anyone. Waiting made you look foolish. Wanting was a weakness.

Yup, that was it, the familiarity was right there. It showed up in the way Malcolm was only giving enough to keep her hopes up, to keep her unstable and indecisive. Just enough to change her mind from "this is over" to "he still cares". She remembered all the times she had been reeled back, in feeling and looking foolish as she watched herself, like an out of body experience, perform. And she still found herself over-functioning, making plans, giving more, and trying to prove she was worth staying for. It was a pattern. And today, in that car with the sandwich in her hand, she whispered to herself, "I'm tired of chasing breadcrumbs and calling it a meal."

Keischa used to say, "I don't care about being picked." She claimed she was too busy, too independent, too focused on her career to be concerned about love and a man. But the truth, the deep-down truth, was she did want love, the engagement of care, consideration, the longing, and sincere deep feeling of being wanted. Being chosen just because of who she was.

But the reality was she didn't want to feel the hurt of abandonment, betrayal, disappointment, or rejection again. The lessons of sacrifice were instilled and etched in her mind early: If you love people, you show up. You give. You aren't selfish. And the big one that she had heard as often as she had heard her name was: It's better to give than to receive.

You take care of the people you love, without question. You sacrifice no matter what.This was a big one, because it wasn't vocalized as much as it was an unwritten, unspoken rule. But you can best believe it was seen. Throughout the generations women sacrificed time and sanity for family, kids, men, job, and anybody but theirself. Even if no one asked, even when tired, even when it isn't reciprocated, sacrifice. And that was the problem.

Now at thirty-six, Keischa was a mother, a hard worker, and everybody's go-to girl. Keischa was exhausted from making room for everyone else. Always showing up. Always available. Always the "strong one." She was tired of carrying that narrative around like a badge of honor. She no longer wanted to be strong, or anyone's sounding board, dumping ground, therapist, or fall guy. She knew, in this moment, she wanted to be seen. She made the decision that pretending she didn't notice when she was hurt, damaged, and overlooked was no longer going to be a part of her play book. The real deal is, she wanted to be chosen. She wanted and needed to be considered. But more than that, more than anything, the ultimate goal was finding someone who believed she was worth the effort.

The Unseen Hunger: Love and Belonging

In Maslow's Hierarchy of Needs, nestled right after food, water, and safety is Love and Belonging. It's right in the middle of his hierarchy because it's the heart of it all. Ok, pause. Let me inject a simple truth before we move on. The pyramid is here as a foundation, but we climb up and down stages to get to actualization. The fact is, healing, health, and life are not linear, but with Maslow's theory we have a guideline to help us move through it.

Ok, back to Love and Belonging. Love and Belonging sounds simple, right? Naw buttercup, buckle up. It's very complex, because it's the place where we move from survival to connection. If your need for love and belonging isn't met, it becomes harder to move toward wholeness. It's where our emotional roots take hold. We need love, intimacy, safety, and consideration. Not just romance.

We form connections throughout the hierarchy: family, sisterhood, friendship, spirituality and community. We begin to recognize that we can have money, homes, and a career yet still feel empty. It is reminiscent of the line in Mahogany (1975), a Back movie featuring legends Diana Ross and Billy Dee Williams (Mannnn, Billy Dee Williams! The absolute sex symbol of our times! Go and check this movie out. Ok, I digress. Back to the story at hand). Billy Dee delivers the infamous line, "Success is nothing without someone you love to share it with." Your spirit and life can still feel empty if your heart, mind, and desires are starving for connection of any kind.

But here's the truth: for so many of us Black women, love hasn't always been safe. Or available. Or easy. We've had to earn it. Prove we were worthy of it. Make ourselves smaller for it. Perform for it. Love and belonging are the longing to feel like you matter. Like someone sees you, connects with you, validates you, and gives you support. It's the safety to be yourself: goofy, messy, anxious, and loveable. The whole 3D you. It's complex, right? You are a whole human being and deserve connections that affirm that fact. We sometimes get pigeonholed into one thing or the other. You've heard people say, "Oh she's street smart, but not book smart," or "She doesn't have feminine energy, she's too masculine." Blah blah blah! Listen, my baby, I know one thing for certain. If toilet paper can be both soft and strong and celebrated for it, I know you can.

We forget to, or were never taught to, or never given the opportunity to show up and take up space. We fit in spaces that feel familiar, safe. We tell ourselves, "Ok, don't do too much." We learn that just being us is not enough, so we don't know what playing out loud or to our talents looks like. We see other people moving in a way that looks like success and praise them, while secretly envying them or wishing we could do what seems easy to them.

Stepping out or up feels scary or inauthentic. Especially when hiding, being behind the scenes, or not getting in the way to stay safe has been our story. This way of protection becomes embedded in who you are. You over-give, become the "yes" girl, silence your needs, and feel like softness has to be deserved or earned. You train yourself to be worthy and valuable because of your actions and loyalty. It becomes a part of who you are, and an intrinsic reward, that people say they can depend on you, that you are nice people, and you will be there to take care of other's needs even to your own detriment.

What the Helley?!! Embracing the notion and narrative that we have to hustle for connection keeps us disconnected, and truthfully, a doormat for people who want the hustle, but decide they don't want what comes with it: support, loyalty, and love for you. It is clear the connection is sold separately or not at all. We learn lessons that we remember from childhood and gather evidence throughout adulthood that leads us to believe whatever narrative we have written for ourselves. The experiences we have seem to validate the mindset of, "See?! I knew if I let my guard down, showed vulnerability, and changed this would happen." And so, begins the cycle of shrinking back, putting up walls, and doing what feels familiar. At least you know the outcome, right?

Ya'll remember attachment theory, right? We discussed it in chapter one and you took the quiz. Let's pause, go back, review, maybe take the quiz again. I was going to do that lil' theme music from Jeopardy, "Do do do do do do do dod doddle do do do do" (or something like that LOL), but y'all might be too young for that (as I date myself). Anywhooo, take your time, remember this book is giving you permission to slow down and value self, so I'll wait while you review. Also, honey pop, remember that you can see yourself in more categories than one and it can change depending on what experiences, trauma, and needs we experience.

Attachment theory helps explain why our attachment style formed from how we were loved (or not) in childhood. If you were the fixer, the caretaker, the "good girl" who kept things together at home, you might find yourself today in relationships where you're always giving, rarely receiving. The attachment in this space looks like anxious avoidant attachment. That's when you crave closeness, but don't trust it. It looks like when you are checking for the exits, even when you are hoping people will stay. It comes from inconsistent love, broken promises, and feeling emotionally abandoned.

Attachment theory tells us about the way we connect with others. Our attachment style shows up in the way we treat intimate relationships and is deeply shaped by what we learned about love as children. While we think about "protecting peace," what we don't understand is that behaviors we choose could be guarding a wound that we don't know how to heal.

We aren't broken or bad at love if our systems sometimes reflect being wired in chaos. Chaos can look like normalcy because we are so used to it, but it shows in inconsistency, abandonment, fear, and betrayal. This chaos makes us scan every relationship for danger and the need for protection. That's not your fault.

But it is something you can heal. For Black women the need for love and belonging gets tangled in survival. We can sometimes become hyper-independent, praised for being strong, the backbone, the glue, and the nurturer. But who are our nurtures? The pressure to always "have it together" keeps us from being vulnerable, from asking for help, from naming our loneliness, or from admitting we still want to be held.

When we don't get that belonging, that sense of closeness, we start to believe it's because we aren't enough. Or that we are the dreaded "too much". Even worse, is the thought that you are "being too hard to love." (What?? How in the blankety blank can someone be too hard to love. Is that even a thing?) That can affect our mental health, change our DNA, and sense of value.

We become experts in detachment. We haven't gotten into detachment yet, but we will. We detach, but deep inside, the longing is still there. The craving for connection. That craving doesn't make us needy. It makes us not want to recognize and accept vulnerability or humanness. The beautiful thing about being, or starting to be, aware is that it opens the door for healing.

Sometimes we chase. We excuse inconsistent behavior. Our needs are ignored and betrayed by ourselves. We make ourselves small just to "fit" into life, friend groups, family, relationships, and situations. Why? Because deep down, we are comfortable with the familiar. It feels safe. And, real talk, we understand it and how to navigate it.

It's not that we don't think we deserve love. It's more of a question of: what does love look like, how do I sustain it, and don't I have to do something to earn it? Everything we get we have had to earn, why would love look different?

The roots of this run deep because of childhood behaviors like helping mom survive by being the coparent, the babysitter to younger siblings, cleaning the house, being good, and practically being the second-in-command. These narratives and stories are ingrained in the story of believing love comes with responsibility, not rest. The definition of rest eludes us when we have not had the luxury of seeing people around us take breaks or felt like it was allowed.

But now, we can start to realize love doesn't feel like labor. Here's the real gag, love and belonging are basic needs. Not extra. Not luxury. Need. It's the deep soul part that so many of us ache for. The part of us that should never require us to abandon self.

"He will quiet you with His love, He will rejoice over you with singing," Zephaniah 3:17.

Real Talk: Love & Belonging for Black Women

Let's tell the truth, sis. Black women are often praised for how well we love others. How we pour, hold, stretch, and sacrifice. But we're rarely taught how to receive love. Or how to rest in it. Or how to say, "This isn't love, it's survival."

Love and Belonging should feel like a safe landing. Not a place where you prove your worthiness, but a place where you are fully, completely, wildly you. When you did not get that safe landing growing up, when affection came with strings or conditions, your body remembers. Even when your mind forgets to offer protection. That's what we call attachment trauma. Early relationships teach us what to expect from love.

If love was safe and consistent, we will tend toward secure attachment.

If love was unpredictable, absent, or came with conditions, we may develop:

- Anxious attachment (cling tightly, fear abandonment)
- Avoidant attachment (keep distance, fear closeness)
- Disorganized attachment (swing between the two)

If your attachment style is anxious, avoidant, or disorganized, it might feel uncomfortable. You might chase emotionally unavailable partners, fear intimacy, or isolate when things get too close. When Attachment Trauma shows up love feels like work you have to earn. You might over-give or shrink yourself to keep the peace. You may settle for crumbs or avoid closeness entirely.

Listen, sis, the good news is that healing work starts with noticing. Then unlearning. Then rebuilding. It's cool. We are doing it together. No need to rush. We arc taking it all in, sip by sip, so it settles in and teaches you the lessons of cultivating the best version of self.

Keischa's Turning Point

That night, Keischa made dinner, but this time she ate first. She sat down, phone face-down, no TV on, no background noise. Just her. It felt strange. Quiet. But in that quiet, she felt a flicker of herself. She texted her friend: "Can we talk about therapy? I think I'm finally ready to heal. You have a therapist I can call?"

Keischa put the phone down and waited for her response, unsure of what to expect, but sure it was time for a change. She'd survived the bottom. She'd fought through to safety. And now, she was learning that love and belonging starts with self. It truly is an inside job. She was moving up the pyramid and didn't have a clue what was on the next level, but it had to be something better. And this time, she wasn't dragging herself to be loved. She was walking toward something new.

Your author friend, here. Let's flashback to my tree analogy and the beauty, the strength, and the growth of upward and downward motion. Yes, remember that we are like trees in many ways, but with one great distinction. We are mobile. We aren't stuck or planted in one place. Ya'll might be saying to yourself that this is a weird segway or an awkward transition to the next chapter. But because you are my peeps, you know there is a purpose. Everything is by design and with a point in mind. This book isn't just a great read, ahemmm, but a teaching tool that is meant to move us up the pyramid and give understanding. It is a motivational tool to move towards developing the best version of you.

So, here's the point. We have to learn that there might never be a perfect time, a perfect transition, or the favored, "I will move when…[insert the distraction or excuse]." It usually sounds something like: when I save some more money, after I develop this plan, when I'm vested in my pension, or when the kids finish school. You know the drill. And don't get me wrong, every excuse can be valid and plausible. However, it doesn't take away the feeling of being stuck. It doesn't stop you from holding tight the belief that you are safe in your present. We stay attached to people, places, and things way too long and then feel as if it's too late to change. We are changing that narrative and perception of time. Side bar: Google people who are doing what you desire to accomplish and their ages. There are seventy-year-olds headed to college and fourteen-year-old millionaires creating businesses.

Eliminate the false concept of time and the belief that you can't. The Bible says, "God is not a respecter of persons." So, if you can find anyone doing what you desire, you can have it as well. Do not let the illusions of, "It is too late for me. I'm too old", or "This is good enough" create a less-than existence and experience for you. We fail to grow when we don't allow ourselves the freedom to even try. Remember Dr Seuss's book "Oh, the places we will go"!

Ok, I'm dating myself, but the movies used to have this little cartoon with dancing and singing snacks – popcorn, candy, hotdogs and soda. It signaled that intermission was almost over and it was time to get back to your seat because the feature was starting. And now back to our scheduled programming.

"Faith is taking the first step even when you don't see the whole staircase."
– Martin Luther King Jr

Chapter Six

Sis, You're Not Angry. You're Hurt.

"Anger is often the mask pain wears when it doesn't feel safe enough to be seen."-Unknown

Keischa

Keischa was pissed, but she didn't know it. She didn't know she was mad about the disrespect of allowing herself to be manipulated at work…again. Her manager was always coming to her with that fake voice, "Hey girl", as if they were friends, "we are short again. Can you possibly do me a favor and stay a little extra for overtime? It would mean the world! I'm strapped and need your help."

Keischa's whole body and mind was screaming, "Girl say NOOO!!! You got stuff to do and places to be. Say no, not this time." That was what her mind was screaming at her, but per usual, the words that came out of her mouth were, "Sure, girl no problem. You know I got you." Pleasant as you please, with that stupid grin. So now, she was outside the grocery store running late for errands and pickups.

As she sat in her car, hands gripping the steering wheel tightly, staring off into space with tears streaming down her face, she just felt like screaming. She wasn't angry about the traffic, nor the missed doctor's appointment (she felt like that was the norm, putting herself last), not even the guy who cut her off in the parking lot yelling obscenities. Those things were only reminders of how she let her boundaries, or lack of them, be crossed over and over. They were the matches. The gasoline was years of feeling unheard, dismissed, and invisible.

What was wild was the lack of control. Usually, Keischa could control her emotions. Today, the tears wouldn't stop, her chest pounded, and she felt like she would break. Today the tears felt like weakness. She didn't recognize this person staring back at her in the rearview mirror. What was worse was not being able to pinpoint the anger.

Sometimes when you can't identify a trigger, a pain point, or a hurt your mind will do it for you. You remember the saying: that was the straw that broke the camel's back. That straw will fall when you least expect it. You won't even see it coming.

The next Monday felt different. Keischa made it through the mundane everyday morning routine of the job by vowing, *"Imma be different today."* She couldn't describe it, but the difference was definitely there. As the day moved forward she was in the breakroom at work, sipping her coffee, trying to make it through the last two hours of a Monday that already felt like Thursday. Her coworker asked an innocent question about a report, and before she could catch herself, Keischa snapped, "Why don't you just read the email like everybody else?!"

She did not even know where it came from. It felt wrong, but a relief at the same time. The harshness of her tone felt like she overreacted, but she couldn't smooth it out or apologize. It just sat there. It wasn't her normal sweet "sure what you need?" self, but no one ever genuinely asked if she is okay. Keischa wasn't okay. She was exhausted, overstimulated, and feeling alone.

She hated how grief hit her after her grandmother died during the pandemic. She couldn't even be there in person because of all the restrictions. *"The pandemic,"* she thought to herself, *"was a wild time."* It was so wild that she had never felt like she was back to herself. Her grandmother, the closest thing to love and sanity in her life, was gone. And it felt like everything and everybody just moved on. Keischa was still grieving her grandmother.

She hadn't had a night of real sleep in months. But to the outside world, when she showed her frustration she was just "difficult", had an attitude, was snide or plain "snappy." Inside, she was suffocating under the weight of expectations she never asked to participate in. She was constantly being asked to lend money, do a favor, help with a bill because the lights were about to be cut off or because, "I'm short this week." Damn!! She wanted to scream, "Do ya'll see me? I'm struggling! I feel like I'm drowning. I'm working hard for me too! I'm not your emergency fund or ATM!"

The first time Keischa realized her, "I'm fine", might be killing her, she was standing at her kitchen sink in the middle of the night debating on calling Malcolm, binge watching a show, or grabbing a night cap to get back to sleep. Her thoughts just hummed along, as she mindlessly poured the drink, but this time her chest felt like it was wrapped in steel bands. Her jaw was tight as her mind replayed an argument from earlier that day with the man she swore she loved. The one who told her she was "too much" when she asked for more intention and communication.

In that moment, allll the consequences of saying I'm fine, showed up in her thoughts. The willingness to keep the peace, to keep the "love", to keep the man showed up as willingness to betray how she felt, what she needed. Usually she would call Malcolm yelling, arguing, cursing. All those adjectives avoided the real one, begging. Begging this man to see her, to stop hurting her. Tonight she couldn't bring herself to yell, to argue. She didn't throw dishes, scream, or slam things, waking the kids up, having to explain what was wrong. She wasn't crying on the outside. She looked like the picture of control, but on the inside she was melting, deflating like the balloons left outside of businesses after grand openings. She felt like a boxer in the last round with nothing left to give. Defeated.

The Neuroscience

So, ya'll already know we ain't going for Psych 101: Lecture 17, but as a mental health expert I will make sure to identify and discuss some bonafide science. LOL! That reminds me of the sitcom "The Big Bang Theory." There is a scene where the character Amy (the actress who plays her is an actual neurobiologist) is making her outgoing answering machine message with her boyfriend and says, "We can't answer the phone right now cuz we kicking science." That was funny to me. Ok, wait. What was my point? Y'all, don't distract me. Oh yeah, the science element. It is important to know that this isn't just an opinion or a fictional story without validation to support how our brains work. So, listen up, buttercups.

Your nervous system remembers love as much as your heart does. If you were raised in a house where love felt unpredictable or unsafe, your body now responds to calm like it's suspicious. This is survival mode. That's because of your **amygdala**. The amygdala is a tiny almond-shaped section deep in the brain that works like a built-in alarm system. It kicks in when we feel threatened either emotionally or physically. It scans for danger and sounds the alarm, dumping stress signals into the body. The amygdala is designed to keep you safe. It's the part of your brain wired for survival.

With every perceived threat your body releases **cortisol**, a stress hormone. Your heart races. Your breathing changes. Your muscles tense preparing you for trouble. But what happens when you've lived too long in survival mode? That alarm can become hypervigilant firing off at the slightest threat even if it's just a loud voice or a dismissive glance.

The amygdala doesn't care if the "danger" is a pit bull chasing you or a partner saying, "You're too sensitive." It reacts the same way. And here's what's important, if the hurt is chronic, your brain keeps you in a low-level fight-or-flight state even when there is no threat. It's like the amygdala is saying, "Girl, we don't do peace. This feels foreign. We need to do something!!"

When cortisol stays elevated too long in your body, it impacts your health causing fatigue, headaches, disrupted sleep, and mood swings. For Black women balancing multiple roles and systemic pressures, this chronic stress is more than an inconvenience. It's a burden that seeps deep into the body.

This is the body-truth we must talk about: Suppressed hurt doesn't disappear. It relocates in the body. It might move into your jaw (teeth grinding), your shoulders (constant tightness), or your stomach (ulcers, IBS). Chronic stress, and high cortisol levels can even impact your immune system, digestion, and memory.

Exploring your body-truth includes understanding how love and attachment are wired into your nervous system. Your **prefrontal cortex** is the thinking brain. Now, she knows better than to react to everything, but when your love history is full of pain your body might sabotage peace to chase chaos. This isn't brokenness. It's the nervous system doing its job. But the job needs a promotion, and that starts with healing how you love.

Your early experiences literally shape how your brain responds to connection, so what happened to your younger self still impacts your older self. Your body doesn't know the difference between danger in 1989 and danger in 2025. But understanding, identifying, and rewiring can keep you from being stuck or defining your present self by your past self. It helps to understand you aren't imagining things. You can identify the triggers that keep you doing what you always have done and finally rewire your brain to give you choices. This helps you to make decisions based on now, instead of what happened in the past.

Let's review this thing called attachment, because it can't get buried. It's important to your growth. Attachment theory tells us that the way you connect to others as adults, especially in intimate relationships, is deeply shaped by what you learned about love as children.

There are four main attachment styles, but you can have a mixture.

1. Secure – You trust love, can give and receive it freely.
2. Anxious – You fear abandonment, over function in relationships.
3. Avoidant – You fear vulnerability, keep love at arm's length.
4. Disorganized – You crave closeness but fear it, often tied to trauma.

If your primary caregivers were consistent and nurturing, your brain developed a healthy attachment system. You gained the ability to trust, seek comfort, and regulate emotions. But if love was inconsistent, unpredictable, or painful, your nervous system adapted, protecting you through hypervigilance, avoidance, or anxious craving.

In brain terms, it's about how the amygdala and prefrontal cortex communicate. When early love is healthy, the brain learns safety in connection. When love is unsafe, the brain's alarm system stays on high alert. When the need for healthy love goes unmet, you feel lonely, isolated, or misunderstood. You might settle for toxic relationships just to feel seen. Or shut down completely because love feels dangerous.

That's why anger often feels bigger than the issue of the moment, your nervous system is time-traveling back to old wounds. Anger can often be traced back to attachment injuries — moments in childhood or early relationships where your emotional needs weren't met in safe consistent ways. The way you react when you are angry can also be tied to your attachment pattern. Remember, these patterns don't just show up in romance. They spill into friendships, work relationships, even parenting.

• Anxious attachment: You might explode out of fear of being abandoned or ignored.

- Avoidant attachment: You might shut down completely, using silence as self-protection.
- Disorganized attachment: You might swing between both, unsure if love is safe at all.

Different strategies, same root: an early history of emotional needs being unmet.

What Does Healthy Love Look Like?

There's so much discussion around healthy love and what it looks like that we need to take a minute to redefine it and give examples of what it might look like. Healthy love isn't just flowers and forehead kisses. Let's get this straight because a lot of times we are under the misconception that healthy love is about never arguing, never feeling hurt, or never having your partner disappoint you.

- Love makes room for your full emotional range.
- Love doesn't punish you for needing reassurance.
- Love stays even when it's uncomfortable.
- Love says: You don't have to earn your rest.
- Love doesn't require anyone's permission or approval.
- Love is mutual respect.
- Love is someone holding your hand when you cry instead of insisting, "You got this, girl."
- Love uplifts without controlling or diminishing.
- Love feels like a safe harbor, not a battlefield.
- Love honors your boundaries and growth.
- Love invites vulnerability without fear.

Healthy love isn't mixed signals and breadcrumbing, having to apologize for having needs, or sacrificing your sanity to avoid abandonment.

Keischa didn't know it yet, but her patterns in love weren't random. They were shaped by her attachment style– the blueprint of her nervous system built from early experiences. Keischa learned anxious avoidant attachment, so she craves closeness but doesn't trust it, always scanning for signs someone might leave and working overtime to keep them close. This comes from inconsistent love, broken promises, and feeling emotionally abandoned although there were always people around. So, when you think of "protecting peace" what you really could be doing is guarding a wound that you don't know needs healing. You become an expert in detachment having a "strong cut off game", but deep inside, craving connection.

Needing connection doesn't make you emotionally needy, "not enough", "too much", or hard to love. It makes us human.

Through the learned narrative of anxious attachment we build our identities in the spaces of survival and silence. We accept love depletion, we serve while starving, digest disrespect and pass this narrative to our children then wonder why we feel so hollow.

The "Cape" and The Strong Black Woman Schema

The "Strong Black Woman" archetype was born in survival. It's the cape our mothers and grandmothers had to wear to keep our communities alive in systems that were never built for our thriving. It was armor against poverty, racism, and erasure. But here's the thing, anything that's never removed becomes a prison or suffocates you.

For Black women especially, society often hands us the "strong" label while quietly stripping away permission to be vulnerable. That gap between being seen as capable and being treated as human can breed frustration that simmers for years.

For Keischa, that prison looked like never letting anyone see her afraid. It meant turning every heartbreak into a project to fix rather than a wound to heal. It meant holding in so much pain that her body became fluent in tension. Here's the thing– this cape thing, this schema, isn't born, it's taught.

As a little girl, Keischa learned to minimize her anger. The conditioning language was loud, clear, and impossible to ignore. Don't be fast, don't have any attitude, don't have a "tone". Questioning was disrespectful and everything seemed hard, dismissive. She learned to shrink down and stay out of trouble. Not out of love and comfort, but in response to control. Control was used as a tool to keep her in her place and conform to the rules.

Being a Black girl meant learning to be good, nurturing, and compliant. It was the key to survival and safety. The cape, heavy and invisible, stitched together from strength, survival, and silence, draped itself over Keischa's small shoulders. She never asked for this "cape" but somehow it had found her. From then on, hurt had to hide behind anger. Vulnerability was dangerous. To show weakness meant risk– risk of being dismissed, risk of being hurt again.

Attachment and the Cape

Attachment theory helps explain why many Black women carry that cape with such fierce pride and reluctance to let go. Our childhoods, sometimes full of unpredictability, sometimes rich with love but wrapped in survival tactics, shape how we connect to others and to ourselves.

- Anxious attachment may make you hyperaware of others' needs, driving you to "fix" everything while ignoring your own hurt.

- Avoidant attachment might lead you to shut down emotions, pretending everything's fine to avoid being vulnerable.

- Disorganized attachment can leave you caught in a push-pull narrative craving connection, but fearing the hurt it might bring.

Keischa feels these patterns in herself, the ways her past shapes her present and how her cape is both her protection and her prison. There is the unspoken rule that pain is something you swallow, not share. The Strong Black Woman narrative often overlaps with these wounds, reinforcing hyper-independence and self-silencing. While these patterns help us survive, they can block us from the very connection that heals.

Maslow's Esteem Needs and Anger

We're climbing the pyramid now. Esteem needs are about self-respect, recognition, and feeling valued. If you've never felt safe to express hurt, your self-worth can get tangled in performance: If I'm perfect, they'll love me. If I speak up, they'll leave. If I speak my truth, I'll be unlikeable.

When you haven't felt healthy esteem that anger shows up and becomes a guard dog. It's fierce and loyal but also exhausting to maintain. But when esteem steps in your anger is heard as pain. Your needs aren't a burden but a bridge.

Keischa

Keischa sat at her desk at work, she had just told a coworker she would fill in for her this weekend. *"Girl,"* she said in her head, *"are you nuts? Have we not been talking about self first?"* Yet, here she was trying to be liked, to be understood, to be acceptable. She sat quietly trying to understand when she decided, or was taught, to be the one who holds everything down, figuring it out all while wearing a smile because, God forbid, she held her own face in any other way than a smile that kept the room comfortable. When did softness and truthfulness become unsafe for her ?

During a meeting in the large, cold, glass-walled conference room, she still thought of how stupid she felt saying yes to her coworkers request. She felt the old tug of tightness in her chest as the same colleague cut her off mid-sentence, dismissing her idea like it was as invisible as the air.

Keischa's throat tightened, and her hands automatically clenched beneath the table. The heat of frustration bubbled up, as she forced herself to focus. Nobody can see her cry. Push those tears back, a lesson she had learned many years ago. What she felt was more than frustration, it was years of being unheard, unseen, and the inability to defend herself without coming off as aggressive, or even worse, needy.

Later that evening, heavy with what happened at work, mom duties, and her constant thoughts of "there has to be something better for me", Keischa laid on the couch in her apartment, pressed her palms to her eyes and wondered, *"Why does this anger feel so big? Why is it always there simmering beneath my skin?"* The answer lies in a map she's never fully seen, Maslow's Hierarchy of Needs at the level called Esteem. It's the place where we feel valued, loved, and confident. Keischa's foundation, unbeknownst to her, was cracked.

Her layer of Love and belonging was been patchy, at best. Every time those needs go unmet, the walls around her heart grow thicker, the cape tighter. Even when faced with the opportunity to drop the cape it still feels unsteady, not safe, like walking up a rotted wooden flight of stairs knowing at any moment you might fall through. Esteem could not be solidly built on a layer like that.

The next morning, Michelle, a good friend, who was always so sweet and caring texted, "Hey Keisch, you been quiet. You good? What do you need?" As usual, Keischa's words didn't match her feelings as she texted her standard answer, "Nah girl, I'm good. Girl, just working," because, real talk, she had no idea of how to answer that question. What was "good"? She shrugged as her mind swirled around the bigger question: What do I need? Her honest response was that she didn't know.

Keischa felt like she had been on "go mode" since she was seven. A memory of getting ready for school at that age flooded back to her. It was an early school morning, like any other, and she was trying to get ready. She was in pain. She had never felt pain like this, ever. It was so bad she couldn't stand straight.

She remembered her mom entering the room as usual with the same morning question, "Girl, what you doing? You gon' be late for school and I'm not taking you." The dialogue, if you could call it that, was dismissive, at best. "Ma, I don't feel good," Keischa remembered saying in a small voice, waiting for comfort, love, and sensitivity. What she got was unexpected. Her mom looked at her and responded quickly, "Well you getting out of here. You'll be alright."

The exchange did something to her. Keischa wasn't mad. Confused and hurt, maybe, but the emotion wasn't anger. She felt empty. Her mom was right, she went to school in pain. It lessened then went away. Lesson learned. That day she learned to swallow her pain and keep it moving. That's how she began to handle the aches and pains of the present. Show up, hold it down, try not to complain out loud, and get it done. But it's little Keischa's pain that shows up in the boardroom, friendships, relationships, and home that never stops aching. And now those dismissive infamous words, "You'll be alright," echo in her spirit every time she feels pain, needs comfort, or needs rest.

Enter Traci

Traci came into Keischa's life in a way that felt accidental. They met at a women's health workshop on a Saturday afternoon. Keischa only went because her coworker kept insisting she needed a "mental health day" and the job was offering comp time for going. So here she was, scanning the room, regretting coming, and ready to bounce. But she grabbed a treat off the snack table and took her seat. *These tarts are delicious. What are these?* she thought as she took a quick picture of her plate to remember to buy some for home, then prepared to listen to the facilitator. She loved how the space felt cozy, warm. Not like a classroom or lecture hall. The chairs were in a semi circle so that everyone could be seen, enveloped. The room was scented by candles but not sweetly, or overbearing. Just enough to breathe in deep and feel like you were at home in front of the fireplace. Something about this felt like a hug, more to the point, intriguing.

To her surprise, and delight, the facilitator was a beautiful Black woman. Her name was Traci, she was in her mid 50s, tall and elegant with beautiful chocolate skin. She looked amazing. The first thing Keischa thought was, "Ok, girl, come through!" but didn't say it out loud because well... anyway, she made a mental note to let sis know later that she was fly. She was the kind of woman who looked like she had her life alphabetized, definitely in order and put together. But when she spoke, her voice carried the same weariness Keischa felt in her bones.

Traci shared her story starting with years of being the "strong one" who held her family together while her own health crumbled. High blood pressure, anxiety, thinning hair, was the cost of never letting down her guard. For Tracie, anger wasn't allowed growing up. In her parent's house, "good girls" kept their voices low and their heads down. She learned to swallow her feelings. That is, until they started showing up in other ways: migraines, back pain, sleepless nights.

Tracie continued, "It's like I was always running on empty," her voice steady but raw. "I thought I was angry at everyone around me, but I was really mad at myself for disrespecting my needs and wants. I was resentful for having to carry everything all alone."

"I thought I was mad at my ex for years," Traci said in the group circle. "Turns out, I wasn't mad. I was hurt. Hurt because he never made space for my fear, my softness, my need to not be the strong one all the time. Hurt that I wasted so much time making excuses and giving passes. I thought I was just angry all the time," she said, "but really, I was tired... so tired of pretending."

Keischa felt her throat tighten. She didn't know this woman, but she felt seen. Keischa didn't realize how much she carried until she met Traci.

Leaving that workshop, Keischa couldn't stop thinking about what Traci said. Hurt, not angry. It kept echoing. She wasn't ready to pour her whole life story out to a stranger yet, she had had the thought of seeing a therapist many times but it never went further than that. But for the first time, therapy didn't feel like an accusation, it felt like an option.

She went home, sat on the couch, and for once, didn't clean anything. She didn't call anyone, didn't turn on the TV for noise, or scroll social media. She just closed her eyes and breathed. In the quiet, she realized something– maybe she wasn't broken. Maybe she was just tired of holding it all. The cape felt a little heavier that night and that was the first sign she might be ready to put it down.

That night, after picking up her children, Haven and Devin, Keischa was frustrated both with the kids, and her mother. She couldn't wait to get the kids in bed and finally lay down. She thought she would be knocked out as soon as her head hit the pillow. Instead, she was lying awake with Traci's words echoing in her mind.

Keischa finally let a crack appear in her armor. Today, the cape felt heavier than ever. To the outside world, she was fine. But inside?

Hurt was the silent current pulling her under, which all too often was mistaken for anger. The quick snaps at work, the tight jaw, the swallowing of what she really wanted to say in family fights with her mother and sisters, the exhaustion that made mornings feel like climbing a mountain. "Sometimes, I don't even recognize myself," she whispered, into the darkness. "I'm not angry, just like Traci said. I'm tired of being tired. I'm hurt and frustrated deep down where no one sees."

Keischa was constantly pretending she could handle it all then finding herself in tears in quiet moments behind closed doors. She pulled out her phone and typed, "Black women therapist near me." Her breath hitched. Fear and hope tangled inside her, *"What if they judge me? What if I'm too much?"* But deeper than that was a whisper she hadn't listened to before, *"Maybe I don't have to do this alone."* Keischa hesitated and quickly closed the tab. That first web search wasn't a full step forward, no, not yet. But, baby, it was an opening, a beginning. The seed was planted.

Maslow's Pyramid and Esteem Built on Performance

When your sense of worth has always been tied to what you do and not who you are, you start building your identity on performance. When Maslow talks about "esteem needs" nestled right in there is respect, recognition, and feeling valued. But if love and belonging were conditional growing up, esteem gets built on over-delivering. You learn false narratives and characteristics that don't mesh with the true version of who you are. Your identity is reduced and you think, "If I'm not strong, I'm nothing." That's not self-esteem. It's self-exhaustion. The weight of conflicting narratives and performance can lead to hurt and frustration that shows up as anger.

When Keischa sits in a conference room, her voice clipped and sharp after being interrupted, yet again. Her heart races, not just with frustration, but with an old, familiar ache, the ache of being unseen, unheard, diminished, disrespected, and exhausted.

What looked like anger was really hurt rooted in childhood memories where emotional safety was scarce. This is the emotional turbulence that Maslow's Hierarchy calls the Esteem tier: feeling valued, respected, and confident in who you are. When these needs go unmet, anger often becomes the loudest voice for hurt that hasn't been healed.

Healing the Hurt Behind the Anger

1. Grounding with the 5-4-3-2-1 Technique

When your body is screaming and your mind races, try this:

- Look around and name 5 things you can see.
- Touch 4 things around you.
- Listen for 3 sounds.
- Identify 2 smells.
- Taste 1 thing — even if it's just the air.

This brings your brain back from survival mode to the present, calming the amygdala's alarm.

2. Emotion Naming and Tracking

Keep a journal where you note emotions. Not just "angry", but what's beneath it — hurt, fear, loneliness, shame etc. Instead of letting anger be your default, try to name what you're really feeling. Writing breaks the chain of reaction and opens a space for healing. This simple act creates space for self-compassion and shifts your brain toward regulation.

3. Self-Compassion Break

When you feel overwhelmed, say to yourself, "I am hurting, and that's okay. I am doing my best." Treat yourself with the kindness you'd give to your best friend.

4. Setting Boundaries

Practice saying "no" without guilt. Your peace matters. The cape doesn't have to be your entire identity.

Reflection

Where do you feel anger that might actually be hurt? What would it look like to give yourself permission to feel that pain without judgment?

Affirmations

- I honor my feelings and give myself grace to heal.
- I release the need to carry burdens that aren't mine alone.

Scripture for Reflection

"He heals the brokenhearted and binds up their wounds." — Psalm 147:3

Chapter Seven

Is the Strong Black Woman a Myth?

"Rest is not a luxury. It's a necessity. You deserve to stop carrying the world on your shoulders." – Iyanla Vanzant

Keischa

Keischa sat in the parking lot of the community center, holding a cold cup of coffee in her hand. It had become a habit to reheat her morning coffee a couple of times before she actually had time to drink it. Her heart was racing like it always did before one of Traci's workshops. The sun was warm and inviting, streaks of light played across the pavement. She could feel the warmth through the window on her shoulders, but it didn't do anything to release the tension she felt between her shoulder blades. Keischa was always the one who looked like she had it all together. From the outside she was polished, well-adjusted, and ready for the world. People often admired her and wanted to emulate her. Her career was intact, she was conditioned to be smile ready, hair always done, kids thriving, and bills paid.

But on the inside, where it mattered, she was unraveling. She spent her nights crying in her pillow wishing and praying for comfort, consideration, and understanding. As she got ready to walk into the workshop, she did what she always did, plastered on a smile and readied herself to lie. She was ready for the "I'm fine" to fall from her mouth right on cue, even though she wasn't.

She felt the familiar quiet panic in her chest begin to rise. But this time Keischa wondered, "What if I..." her phone vibrated several times interrupting her thoughts. The usual suspects came through, school reminders, work tasks, friends' updates, a reminder that someone still needed to borrow a couple of dollars. And one from Malcolm. *"Hmm"*, she thought, *"Malcolm. I can't deal with him right now. I'll call him after the workshop."*

Looking at the text message from Malcolm Keischa read, "Baby, I miss you. It feels like I can't breathe without you. You are my peace. Can I see you?" Same ole line. She would usually be excited, happy to see his text and read those words, but today the text reminded her of a conversation she had had with her mom.

"Keisch", she would say, "don't be a fool, baby. Don't trust nobody too much. Even love will betray you, if you let it." Her mother's voice was sharp, clipped, and heavy with her own disappointments. That warning had become what Keischa lived by, her survival code. It explained why she couldn't let Malcolm go, even though deep down inside she knew he was more illusion than promises.

Inside, the workshop smelled of coffee, lavender, and vanilla candles. Sweet smells of baked muffins and treats lingered in the air. The unassuming air of quiet anticipation. Traci was walking around the semi-circle of folding chairs, placing affirmation cards on each seat. As usual, she was humming softly, almost angelic. The sound of people chattering exhibited a mixture of nervous energy and excitement. The room always felt like a subtle invitation to relax and breathe. It felt familiar and brought comfort to Keischa.

Traci's workshops always put her deep in thought, questioned her perspective, and validated her needs. This time, as Keischa poured a fresh cup of coffee, she felt different, like an edge of possibility was pressing against her ribs. It felt like she was changing. Traci's words were penetrating and had started to reach places Keischa had thought she had sealed away. She was nervous, not because she didn't want to be there, but because she knew every session peeled back a little more of her armor. Here's the thing though, today, she wasn't sure she had the strength to peel back anything. But then again, wasn't that the reason she was here?

Keischa was jarred out of her thoughts by a young Black woman. She had a cocoa complexion, looked to be about 30ish wearing a messy bun, dressed casually, but chic, energetic, and beautifully made up. She was masterfully juggling her purse, computer bag, briefcase, and a banana walnut muffin. All while squatting down to clean up the coffee she spilled on the floor.

She suddenly beamed a beautiful, toothy, brilliant white smile and said, with all eyes on her, "Carry on, everybody, there's nothing to see here." Keischa was instantly fascinated. Where did she get the confidence to not care what people thought? She walked over and helped her and then hurried to her seat as the workshop began. When this stranger took her seat next to Keischa she said, "Thanks, sis. I appreciated you helping me with that mess. You ready to do some unraveling?" Keischa immediately noticed how her pretty brown eyes twinkled. Keischa whispered. "Yeah, No worries." It was an instant clique.

Simone

Simone Parker is thirty-two, works in nonprofit management, and oversees programs for at-risk youth. She is fiercely independent, but quietly exhausted from carrying too much. The "too much" she always carried that nobody noticed. She has no kids, which makes her an easy target for favors, because, of course, no kids means "free-time" to everyone else.

However, it's cool because her love flows freely and naturally to her nieces, nephews, and younger cousins. Her apartment smells of fresh linen, cinnamon, take out, and candles. Her prized possession was her bookcase. It was filled with worn novels by Toni Morrison (The Bluest Eye), Audre Lorde (Sister Outsider), and bell hooks (All About Love). These women were her idols—- strong, Black, creative, intelligent, writers, activists, and award-winning women who shaped her understanding of herself and the world.

Simone grew up in the middle of two sisters with a single mother who worked tirelessly as a postal worker. Growing up, she was the one that was often overlooked. She wasn't the shining academic star like her oldest sister, Carla, who graduated from college with honors and was praised for her hard work. She wasn't the baby of the family, like Mya, who was coddled and adored (code for spoiled) for doing nothing but being little and cute.

Simone learned that her space in the family was faded. Nothing big, nothing small just there. She learned that she was insignificant. She learned that it was easy to avoid conflict by following the rules and overlooking things. She learned to smile even when she felt like she was unseen. That is, unseen until her mother needed something, like someone to talk to. Even if the conversation was beyond her young years, Simone was the sounding board. Or when her help was needed to prepare meals or clean the house.

Simone grew up fast realizing there was value in keeping things in order and being a confidant. Inside, she harbored a strong resentment that continued to brew, but Simone kept that part buried, or so she thought. Her resentment became evident through her communication. The sarcasm, sharp tongue, and quick wit were masks for her unhealed wounds that were never addressed.

Her boundaries were blurry, if you could say that. The real definition of her boundaries was... well, non-existent. How could she have boundaries when there were no defined roles in her life, no concrete rules, and constant silent chaos and negative patterns. Simone wrestled daily with loneliness and people's perception that she had "it all together". She had spent most of her twenties chasing stability. The learned behavior of stretching herself often led to overexertion and defining herself as someone who was fiercely loyal.

This self-defined loyalty wasn't reciprocated or founded in anything particular, mainly just time. Simone gave loyalty where it didn't necessarily fit. She carried responsibilities that weren't hers to carry and became the nurturer, the fixer, and the person who felt exhausted, but didn't have a way to step off the hamster wheel. So, she just kept going, kept giving, being the manager of other people's feelings, and took on the self-appointed task of making sure that everybody else was ok. Responsibility became her identity.

She had become the dependable one, not because she wanted to, but because it had begun to feel comfortable and normal– like she had to fulfill this role. But somewhere along the way she found out she was never taught to be the one to ask for help. She became the "I'm here person". The, "Hey Simone, you got time to do me a favor?" person. The, " Hey friend, you got a minute?", "Hey girl, sorry to ask again but...", "Hey girl, I hate to ask but I'm short...," person. The, " Hey Simone, I need..." person.

That's why she was here at this workshop. She needed answers and change because what she was doing wasn't working. In fact, it was draining and she felt like she was drowning. She was tired of being invisible. Her exhaustion was deep and hidden, yet she carried it so that nobody saw the real her. She was never asked if she needed help, mainly because she was always perceived as doing good. What they didn't see were the private breakdowns, the migraines that stole her weekends, the tears she hid sitting in the bathroom, or the loneliness that comes with being strong and never having the luxury of falling apart.

Workshop

Traci stood in front of the group. The room was quiet except for the hum of the fridge. Her voice was calm, but commanding. It filled the room. "Thriving", she said, "isn't just surviving. It's leaning into your softness, your vulnerability, and the parts of yourself you've been told are unsafe. It's the love you've been withholding from yourself. It's learning that you can't confuse struggle with love."

"Today," she began, "we're talking about the third level of Maslow's Hierarchy: Love and Belonging. Now, I don't want you to think of this as some abstract theory. Remember, Maslow's Hierarchy helps to clarify why you feel like something is missing. Even if your safety and physiological needs are mostly met, if your needs in the third step of Love and Belonging aren't, you feel incomplete."

Traci walked to the easel where the pyramid was sketched and wrote the words "love and belonging" slowly on the whiteboard. "But baybee, here's the catch: for many Black women, survival has been the floor we've been stuck on. Our mothers and grandmothers fought to keep the lights on, to make ends meet, and keep food on the table. Love wasn't a priority. It often came last. But let's not get confused, we aren't talking about just romantic love. It's friendships, family, community, and the people who see you and give you space to rest. Let's think about the moments you felt like you had to earn love. Or the times when belonging felt like it came with conditions," Traci slowly added. "Attachment theory explains why we repeat patterns that hurt us: over-functioning, withdrawal, and mistrust of closeness."

The room grew still. Traci paused and let her eyes sweep the room. "We keep attachment patterns close and defined. A person whose attachment was shaped in a house where love was inconsistent or survival came first, feels belonging is dangerous. You can't build intimacy on a shaky foundation."

Keischa shifted in her seat and glanced at Simone who looked uncomfortable. She looked at her feet as the words felt heavy and sank in. Traci turned toward Keischa, "Would you mind sharing what survival looks like for you?"

Keischa swallowed hard, but felt safe and nodded. "I've always been the one who held things together. Since I was a kid, I felt like if I didn't do it, it wouldn't get done. Even in relationships, I over-give. I stay longer than I should. I call it loyalty, but..." she continued, "if I'm real, it's fear. I fear that if I stop, everything, including me, will fall apart."

Tears streamed down her cheeks. The group nodded and murmured in agreement. She saw Simone shift in her chair. Simone chimed in, her voice was low but sharp, "I get that, sis. But for me, it's like I just stopped expecting anything. From my family, from men, even from my friends. I tell myself I don't need anybody, but inside I'm screaming for someone to see me. To care, to say, 'Nah, F that. I got you!" Honesty and knowiness hung heavily in the room.

Traci acknowledged the stories and the women who were vulnerable enough to share. She continued to share her own story. Keischa loved this part. The part that felt real, warm, and inviting. Traci wasn't just a therapist or a lecturer, but a real person that she could connect with. Traci continued, "As a girl, I thought perfection was the ticket to safety. I got straight A's, did chores without being asked, never broke rules or talked back. I thought I had to be flawless to deserve peace. But therapy, years later, taught me otherwise: love without conditions is the foundation of thriving."

For some reason that resonated with Keischa, and she scribbled it in her notebook. She replayed the sentence over in her head, *"Love without conditions is the foundation of thriving."* Traci continued in her calm voice and easy manner, "I used to think thriving meant keeping it together, but thriving isn't about perfection. It's about wholeness. For years, I believed love meant proving my worth, so I chased jobs, degrees, and relationships. I looked good on paper, but when I was finally alone with myself, I didn't know how to be loved without performing. Honestly, I'm not even sure I knew how to be loved, period. That was my attachment wound speaking."

Ok, pause. You are doing an amazing job, Ms. Traci, but we can't just rush past this piece. Let me step in for a quick moment, y'all. Listen, when we talk about attachment wounds there needs to be context and definition because this can get sticky. Ok, let's get into it.

We know wounds, psychological and physical, need to be looked at and assessed to know the care that is needed before they are cleaned, bandaged, and finally healed. Similarly, when love and belonging are fractured, or disrupted, self-esteem becomes shaky because you are trying to build confidence without a healed foundation.

The unmet emotional need for safety, love, and connection that should have been given to you by your primary caregivers, or "your person" in an intimate relationship, brings with it the fractured foundation of the unhealed attachment wound that Ms.Traci was speaking about before I interrupted.

An unhealed attachment wound can be from not being seen or understood in the past, and can make it hard to feel that it's safe to be vulnerable or that we are loveable and worthy in the present. The negative effects can include hiding vulnerability and tenderness because, let's face it, there have been times when you let down your guard and had vulnerability used against you.

The love fracture (attachment wound) can show up as pouring into others, overextending, and carrying emotional labor, while hoping and praying that it will be reflected back to you by those that you give to the most. And lastly, you mistake survival for love, which means you are loyal in relationships and incorrectly perceive that as connection. Okay, y'all, let's get back to this workshop. Take it away, Traci.

"When I was twenty-four," Traci continued, "I thought I was in love. He was the man who said all the right things, but he was also the man who disappeared when I needed him most. I stayed because of my attachment style. Anxious and hungry for reassurance, I believed crumbs were a feast. They say to a starving man a cracker will seem like a steak dinner. It took me years to realize that I deserved more. At this point in my life, shoot, I deserve, and require, the whole loaf."

The women chuckled, but they also nodded. Some averted their eyes to hide tears. Traci turned back to the board and the sketch of Maslow's pyramid. Traci wrote with a pretty green marker "Maslow's Hierarchy of Needs + Attachment Theory".

"Here's the truth," she said in a sweet, gentle way. "As Black women, many of us are stuck in survival mode. We meet the basic needs for safety, housing, and finances keeping our families alive. We think we don't have time for love, rest, or joy. But thriving requires climbing this ladder. And attachment theory explains why some of us cling to relationships or habits that keep us on the lower rungs repeating the same day over and over."

Traci paused, then turned to another participant directly, "What rung are you on, sis? Survival, Belonging, Esteem, or moving toward self-actualization?"

The lady spoke a little too loudly, "I think...I've been stuck between Belonging and Esteem. I chase people who don't choose me, hoping it'll make me feel like I'm desirable, like I'm worthy of approval." Then ending her thought almost in a whisper she added, "Like I'm enough."

"That's honest," Traci replied softly. "Survival strategies that are learned in childhood play out in adult life. This is where the work begins to change those learned patterns."

After the workshop Keischa had so much on her mind. She had finally decided it was time to book a one-on-one individual therapy session with Traci. The workshop had brought up a lot of emotions, flashbacks, and feelings she had pushed down and forgotten about.

That night Keischa sat on the edge of her bed, staring at the familiar cracks in the ceiling. They weren't just cracks in the plaster; they were maps of her survival. Each jagged line seemed to trace her story, the late nights worrying about bills, the mornings spent rushing children out the door, the silence she carried after heartbreak. She closed her eyes and breathed deeply. She remembered something from the workshop that Traci said, "You cannot thrive while holding your breath." Those words settled in Keischa's chest like a heavy truth she had known, but never dared to name, or allowed herself the luxury to speak out loud.

That night, Keischa dreamed of her mother. She was eight years old, watching her mom at the kitchen sink, tired eyes, chipped nails, humming off-key.

"Keisch, I know you don't be listening, but hear this babe. Don't ever let no man think he's doing you a favor by loving you," her mother said. "But don't you go thinking you're too good for anybody either. Love is compromise."

She woke suddenly and lay in the dark thinking of the lesson her mother shared in the dream. It was a confusing lesson, one that left Keischa straddling between self-worth and self-abandonment. Malcolm and his behaviors fit the blueprint of confusion perfectly. Oh, shoot! She remembered she had meant to call him back. That call was going to be a back-and-forth argument with tons of questions that she didn't feel needed answers. And it brought up feelings of being questioned as a child. Not to mention, she was in no mood to have a battle that always ended up going nowhere.

Malcolm Daily

Malcolm Daily was the kind of man you noticed twice. The first time for his looks, the second time for the way he carried them. At thirty-six, he had the sort of striking handsomeness that could either intimidate or disarm, depending on how close you stood. His skin was smooth, chestnut-brown, and glowed even under harsh lighting. His beard was shaped sharp enough to look intentional, but not vain. His deep-set eyes, that almost seemed midnight black, had soulfulness behind them. He had a way of sizing up a room before he said a word, and when he finally smiled, dimples framed his face like they were carved there for the very purpose of giving women a place to land their eyes.

Malcolm wasn't tall enough to be a star basketball player, but he was tall enough to command a space with a frame broad from years of half-consistent gym routines. He liked sneakers, but questioned if he was too old to be a sneaker head. He always rocked a clean haircut and cologne that lingered long after he left, but in a good way. A way that made you want to follow that scent to wherever he landed. He didn't have to work hard to get attention; he was the kind of man people gave it to freely, almost without realizing.

But attention wasn't the same as love. And that's where Malcolm struggled. He grew up watching his father, Leonard Daily, walk in and out of their house, and his mother's life, like love was optional. Leonard was charming, magnetic, and worked hard when he felt like it, but he also carried the kind of restlessness that made him unreliable. Malcolm hated that as a boy. He hated waiting on promises that didn't always come true, hated watching his mother hold the family together with sheer determination. But as much as he swore he wouldn't be like his father, some of those same patterns lived inside him.

Even now, stability wasn't his strong suit. His looks and personality were what people were drawn to. He was able to use these qualities to get by in life. Still, he had a way of drifting in and out of focus. One minute he'd be present, taking you out, checking in, holding you close. The next, he'd be distracted, questioning whether you really saw him, whether he was really getting what he deserved. He craved attention, the way some people crave air, and when he didn't feel it, he pulled back. Not because he didn't care, but because inconsistency felt familiar.

And women? Women weren't hard for him. Relationships came easy. Well, not really relationships. Let's just say "women". Let's make that the starting point. The conversations, the laughter, the late-night drives with music low and his hand on her leg? It felt so natural. He knew how to show up and make a woman feel chosen. But what came after was a question mark. Could he stay? Could he anchor? Could he withstand the silence when the shine of the new relationship wore off? Malcolm felt like he had tried.

His mothers voice constantly echoed in his head with each new relationship. "Son," she would say, "what are you doing with your life? This is crazy. A new woman every few months. I hope you don't turn out like your father. I worked too hard to get you to be better."

Two years earlier, he had been in a serious relationship with Patrice. She was a woman ten years his senior. At forty-six, sharp-minded, and put together, Patrice was the kind of woman who had lived enough life not to play games. She was direct, handled her business, and thought Malcolm's charm was cute, but not a meal ticket. For a while, he liked it. It was so attractive. It was a space he had never known or felt. She challenged him, made him grow up, and steadied him. But eventually, the differences caught up. Patrice wanted stability and consistency. Malcolm wanted to feel like he was enough without always being pressed to deliver.

Their relationship eventually ended, but not before leaving Malcolm with the one thing he treasured most: his daughter, Malia. Two years old now, Malia was Malcolm's soft spot, the place where all his contradictions melted away. She had his eyes, big and searching, and his smile, coveted dimples and all. When she laughed, it was contagious. It was the kind of sound that made Malcolm believe in redemption. He adored her, bragged about her to anyone who'd listen, showed off her pictures before anyone even asked.

But co-parenting wasn't smooth. Patrice was older, wiser, and tired of inconsistency. She didn't want to hear Malcolm's excuses about being too busy or too tired. She wanted him to show up every time, the way a father should. And though Malcolm loved Malia with his whole heart, his in-and-out ways sometimes showed up – even there. He was present more often than not, but the shadow of his father lingered. It was a constant reminder of what he didn't want to become, but he felt pulled toward it anyway.

Malcolm wasn't a bad man. He was complicated. He was magnetic. He was flawed. He was every bit the kind of man you could fall for before you realized it. It wasn't because he lied about who he was, but because he could look different day to day. And for women like Keischa, women who still wrestled with patterns of attachment and belonging, a man like Malcolm was familiar. He felt like home, even when home hadn't always been safe.

Keischa

Keischa lay in bed staring at the ceiling fan, the slow blades slicing through the late-night silence. Her phone buzzed on the nightstand, as usual, but this time she was sure it was Malcolm. One thing for certain, he didn't like being left on read. His name lit up the screen like a neon sign she couldn't ignore. She let it ring. Tonight, he was on Do Not Disturb. Just for tonight, she needed her breath back.

Her chest rose with the weight of the workshop, Traci's piercing words, and Simone's unexpected vulnerability. For the first time in a long while, she wasn't consumed with running after someone else's needs. She felt the faint stirrings of her own.

Her fingers hovered over her phone and instead of opening Malcolm's thread, scrolling social media, or goggling a new brunch spot, she texted

Simone, "Hey, girl. Coffee in the morning? My treat." She stared at the screen until the little bubbles popped up. Those little bubbles can trigger an anxiety attack, LOL! You start to feel like they don't want to talk to you. Especially when they disappear, or your imagination tells you they can't figure out the correct phrase to let you down gently. Or those bubbles can give you the satisfaction that the person you texted values you enough to text right back.

"Absolutely, " was Simone's eager reply. "9 a.m. Don't be late." The text sent elation and joy through Keischa. "By why?" she thought. "Girl, calm down. It's just coffee." A smile crept across Keischa's face. The kind that wasn't forced or hiding behind "I'm fine." It was the beginning of something fragile and new – sisterhood and connection. The kind of connection that carried an air of possibility Keischa had been craving.

Keischa had one final thing she needed to do now before she changed her mind. Tapping on a bookmarked website in her phone's internet browser app, she hurried to Traci's one-on-one therapy session schedule. She scrolled until she found an opening. Her thumb hovered. Heart pounding. Then she scheduled it. After seeing the notification of the confirmation email pop-up, she opened her calendar app, the one she had avoided for weeks because it was filled with meetings, bills, and reminders that life moved on whether she was ready or not. She typed: Individual Therapy with Traci: Thursday, 3:00 PM.

For the first time in a long time, she didn't feel like she was drowning. Exhaustion was still there, yes, but it was paired with a flicker of relief. She didn't have to figure it all out tonight. She just had to show up. And so, with Malcolm silenced, Simone confirmed, and Traci scheduled, Keischa pulled the covers up to her chin. For once, sleep wasn't the enemy. It was the promise of rest and maybe, just maybe, renewal.

Mental Health Strategies: Moving Toward Vulnerability & Healing

1. Write a Vulnerability Letter

- Pick one person in your life (past or present) you've struggled to open up to.
- Write a letter sharing what you've held back, your fears, your disappointments, your longing.

You don't have to send it. The healing begins with acknowledging your truth on paper.

2. Attachment Wound Work through a Reparenting Exercise
- Close your eyes and picture your younger self at the age you first felt abandoned or unseen.
- Imagine sitting with her. What would you say? How would you comfort her?
- Write a short script offering her the words you needed then.

This builds self-compassion and begins repairing attachment wounds.

3. The Circle of Trust Exercise
- Draw three concentric circles on a piece of paper.
- Label them: Inner, Middle, and Outer.
- Write names of people you know that match the meaning of each circle.

Inner Circle: write people safe for your deepest truths.

Middle Circle: write those you share selectively with.

Outer Circle: write acquaintances or people who don't get access to your vulnerability.

This helps you lean into vulnerability with boundaries, protecting your heart while still opening it.

4. Body Scan for Emotional Safety
- Lie down or sit comfortably.
- Slowly scan your body from head to toe noticing tension, discomfort, or ease.
- Place your hand on your chest and whisper, "I am safe to feel. I am safe to be me."

This builds awareness of where emotions live in your body and offers grounding when vulnerability feels overwhelming.

Affirmations for This Chapter
- I am worthy of safe love and honest connection.
- I can open my heart without losing myself.
- My voice matters, my truth matters, I matter.
- Every step toward vulnerability is a step toward freedom.

Scripture for Reflection

"My grace is sufficient for you, for my power is made perfect in weakness." 2 Corinthians 12:9

Chapter Eight

What We Didn't Know Did Hurt Us

"The most common way people give up their power is by thinking they don't have any." – Alice Walker

Keischa

Keischa woke up with a knot in her stomach and a throat full of words she hadn't yet found a way to articulate. Her house was quiet except for the usual comforting sounds like the hum of the refrigerator, the soft rattle of the heat blowing in the vents, and the distant sounds of the morning neighborhood waking up. She lay on her back, and watched the patch of light on the ceiling turn from blue to gold, like a slow promise.

Her thoughts drifted to Malcolm. The way he entered her life had been both magnetic and messy. He was charming, handsome, the type of man who didn't need to chase attention because it naturally flowed to him. Yet, his in-and-out pattern always kept her guessing. She knew this pattern mirrored patterns she'd seen in childhood, the moments of love, then withdrawal, leaving her wondering if she was enough. Last night Malcolm had called several times. She'd let it ring, her body too tired to match his energy. Her phone was on the nightstand, and with a lethargic swipe she picked it up.The notification blinked: (1) voicemail. She pressed play.

"Keisch…," His voice was low, rough, a mix of Hennessy (his favorite) and regret. "I don't even know why I'm calling. It's just, damn, I miss you. You got me feeling like I'm the only one out here still trying. I see you, I do, but sometimes it feels like you ain't got space for me. And I know I pull back. I know. But I don't want to lose you. I just… I don't know how to stay when it feels like I'm the only one fighting for us. I need you."

Silence. Then a shaky breath. Click.

A few hours later, Keischa sat across from Simone at a small quaint café with not too many people or foot traffic. They were nicely nestled in the corner. She loved it here. It was private, but not secluded. The café had the wonderful smell of fresh bagels, croissants, and fresh roasted coffee. The sound of espresso beans being grounded was mesmerizing. She loved the quotes and affirmations on the walls, bright colors, and comfortable seating. An added bonus was the mugs, *"Eclectic,"* she thought. They were all different colors, shapes, and sizes. They all carried different personalities. Today she was sharing one of her private joys with Simone.

Her coffee sat untouched, steam curling upward in lazy circles begging to be noticed. Simone calmly stirred her tea with the kind of absent-minded rhythm that told Keischa she was either really calm, or her mind was a million miles away. It was wild that they didn't have to perform or put on for each other. Keischa could still feel the collective vulnerability they shared.

Simone interrupted her thoughts with a well-placed, "What up girlie? You seem a little rattled. Still thinking about the workshop? I think it's going to get deep. My girl, Traci, going in today about them attachment wounds. Buckle up, buttercup!" Her laugh was so contagious. Keischa loved it, and it always came with that twinkle in her eye.

"No," Keisha said quickly. "I mean…yeah, that too. But no, I was thinking about Malcolm. Listen to this voicemail he left me last night." After replaying the voicemail, Keisha looked to Simone for guidance and support. "What you think?" she asked, staring and holding her breath.

Simone

Simone let out a slow breath. In that moment, Simone realized that she and Keischa had grown closer. She began to recognize patterns in Keischa that she saw in herself. Their friendship had begun with shared survival stories, but had grown into much more than that, very quickly. She felt the pain that Keisha was feeling, the pain of being exhausted with...well, with life.

Simone continued, "Listen Sis, you can't keep letting half-healed people with their half-hearted promises manipulate you, write your story, or determine your worth. Remember when Traci said, 'You don't deserve the crumbs you deserve the whole loaf'? You deserve more than a drunk voicemail at 2 A.M. when there is nothing better to do. That voicemail doesn't equate to commitment. Damn, you couldn't even call that love. You deserve real conversations and consideration. I get you love him, but don't let his wounds keep reopening yours. Don't shoot the messenger, girl. I'm just saying," she said with her usual casual, but serious enough that you took heed, tone. "Ok girl, let's get outta here. We got to get to this workshop to keep us moving up that ladder."

Keischa smiled a quick smile and thought to herself, *"That was blunt and sharp, but honest."* Before these workshops, her guard would have been up, she would have been offended, and defensive. Today she thought, *"Girl, that's exactly what I needed to hear."* But out loud said, "I know that's right! Let's go."

Traci's Workshop

Keischa and Simone sat in Traci's workshop, surrounded by Black women who carried stories etched in their bones. This session was called Healing Attachment Wounds. Traci had mentioned attachment wounds in a previous session, but believed the concept needed to be explained more, grounded, and given more weight. So, here they were, ready to learn more about what makes us "tick."

The community center smelled of coffee, lavender, and the lemony sweep of the janitor's cleaner. Keischa loved the comfort and familiarity of this room. Traci stood at the whiteboard; marker uncapped in her hand like a magic wand. The circle was full tonight. There were women of every background and age. She felt their hum. There was a specific energy that was felt when Black women gathered. She also loved this room's imperfect ritual: the clink of ceramic mugs, the shuffle of feet, the twinge of relief when someone else asked the question you'd been too ashamed, or afraid, to voice.

Traci began, eyes scanning the room to make sure it was a safe place for knowledge, clarity, and vulnerability. "Let's begin with this," she said softly, but with presence and command. "I have talked about my attachment wound briefly, but wanted to review the concept more deeply for understanding. First a reminder, attachment is more than romance. It is the thread that is woven through family, friendships, work, and self-perception." She inhaled deeply and began, "Attachment wounds are the wounds that show up. They are about what happened to you. They are about what we learned to expect from love."

On the board, she wrote: ATTACHMENT WOUNDS. Under that she highlighted four bullet points:

- Fear of Abandonment
- Fear of Rejection
- Avoidance of closeness
- Need for control

Then she continued, "These are some of the fingerprints of attachment wounds. They don't show up randomly. They come from our earliest connections: our mothers, fathers, caregivers, the people who taught us, intentionally or not, what love feels like and looks like."

"Attachment wounds," she said, "are how our early blueprint for connection maps onto our adult life." She drew Maslow's pyramid on one side and, next to it, a quick diagram of the attachment styles:

Maslow's Pyramid/Ladder of Needs: Basic safety → Love and Belonging → Esteem → Self-actualization.

This is how your early relationships teach you to get your needs met:

- Secure- caregivers were predictable and attuned. You learn as a child that needs will be met. As an adult, you tend to trust and balance intimacy and autonomy.

- Anxious (preoccupied) - inconsistent caregiving teaches you, as a child, to be hypervigilant for love. As an adult, you tend to seek outside reassurance, to over-give, and to scan for threats of abandonment.

- Avoidant (dismissive)- caregivers were emotionally unavailable. As a child, you learned to be self-sufficient and to dismiss needs. As an adult, you protect yourself through emotional distance and independence at all costs.

- Disorganized- caregiving was frightening or erratic. As a child, there was a high level of uncertainty around attachment. As an adult, this may show up as erratic closeness, or avoidance, often tied to trauma.

"This is not Psych: 101," she added, smiling. "This is survival science. When your primary caretakers couldn't give consistent safety, your nervous system learned patterns to keep you alive." She tapped the pyramid. "Safety is at the base. When that's shaky, belonging gets tricky. When belonging is built on effort, or shame, esteem withers. And the top, self-actualization, becomes hard to reach. This is the space where we name the science and the story."

"Let's weave in the Attachment styles. Remember we did the quiz? Review if you need to. Attachment wounds often strike at the Love and Belonging step. If you learned that love was conditional, (ex:learned I must be useful, quiet, perform), your adulthood looks like trying to buy belonging by performance. This keeps esteem shaky, because true healthy esteem is built on being valued for being, not doing, and self-actualization stalls because the energy is siphoned to proving.

Traci stopped, looked around the room, and declared, "Listen y'all, that was a lot of information. So, let's take a break. Breathe, walk around, laugh, and stretch." When we reconvened, Traci did a little makeshift dance and sang loudly, "Ya'll ready for this?!" from the Space Jam Theme, which she said aged her. The group laughed and got comfortable.

She continued, "For Black women, the expectation of the 'strong Black woman' often cements a need to avoid vulnerability, or creates a space of anxious over giving. Healing the attachment wound requires both somatic interventions and relational experiments. **Somatic interventions** are a type of body-mind therapy. It helps process and release trauma, stress, and negative emotions by focusing on the physical sensations and bodily responses." Traci paused and chuckled, " Those are long definitions. Somatic interventions are the therapy that helps the nervous system feel different. And **relational experiments** are therapeutic interventions that prove that new behaviors yield different results.

Keischa felt a hot truth press under her ribs. Her earlier experiences had been a trade for belonging. Simone's oath to not be needy had been a strategy for esteem or, at least, the illusion of it.

Traci asked, "Can someone tell us about a recent time they felt their attachment pattern show up?" Hands rose. The room leaned in. Traci invited Keischa and Simone to speak first.

Keischa's voice trembled, "I...text my guy friend Malcolm when I'm anxious. Even if I know he won't answer. I tell myself it's okay to check on him, but really, I'm checking for proof that I matter."

Simone, in a quieter register, said, "I take on extra things for friends. I tell myself it's helpful, but when the returns aren't equal, I get furious and then I do nothing." Her laugh came out small and brittle, not like the laugh Keischa had become accustomed to hearing.

Traci nodded in agreement and understanding. "That's it, these are the ways the wound shows up. The brain rehearses the same script until we give it a new cue." She guided the group into a paired exercise. "Turn to your neighbor, say in two minutes how someone left you feeling abandoned as a child, and then say how that pattern shows up now. No counseling. No fixing. Just us supporting, understanding, and witnessing."

The room folded into pairs. As the women began talking, some voices broke and some hands rose to their mouths in a knowing way. A woman across the circle, Tamika, said through clenched teeth, "My grandmother told me girls didn't complain, they worked out their problems. And kept their relationship problems to themselves. So, I never told anyone how my boyfriend treated me; the degrading, the cheating, or the lack of affection. So when he left, everyone assumed I did something to this great guy. It had to have been my fault. I thought silence was the way to keep love." The woman's voice broke into a sob. Her partner placed her hand on her back without explanation. No words were needed.

During the pair-share, something shifted. Keischa, with her hands shaking, said something she hadn't intended to share aloud, "I learned that love is earned through being useful." Simone's eyes filled and she reached across the circle to squeeze Keischa's hand. Another woman upon hearing Keischa's words, started crying. The room responded with a sound like a window opening and a fresh wind blowing in. Traci paused and let the room breathe. "When we name it," she said, voice small but clear, "we start to rewire."

In a louder voice for the group she began to frame the learning. "This is how the wound gets triggered. A partner withdraws, and you chase. You reinforce the behavior of chasing because sometimes, in your mind, it works. Your mind gobbles up this data and correlates it to a win. You feel that you performed enough to save the relationship. Or you withdraw to avoid pain, and that becomes the reinforcement to stay distant because distance seems like protection, survival. That's the loop. We break the loop by recognizing the pattern, naming the wound, and slowly rewriting the script."

She turned back to the group. "Who here has ever felt like love comes with conditions? That you had to earn it, perform for it, settle for it, or hold it tight so that it doesn't slip away?" Hands slowly lifted, one by one. Keisha's hand was first. Simone's was the second.

"What about relationships outside of romantic ones?" Traci continued, "How many of you have stayed in friendships, or relationships, because you feared being alone? Even when you felt unseen, unheard, and devalued?" Simone shifted, raising her hand.

Traci noticed. "Simone, would you be willing to share?" Simone cleared her throat, searched the room for safety, closed her eyes and spoke. "The way I grew up, it always seemed like I was easily forgotten, overlooked, and an after-thought. I found myself being the peacekeeper. I made sure everybody was good, and tried to keep everyone in line. That was my way of showing my value. I didn't want to get overlooked. So, now in friendships, I over-do. I always show up, make people feel needed and wanted through gift giving and being available. I give rides, money, time, and if I'm being honest, sometimes at my own detriment. I'm terrified if I stop, people won't stick around."

"That's a wound," Traci said gently with her hand on Simone's shoulder. "Your belonging got tied to usefulness. That's not so uncommon for Black women. Many of us were taught our value is in what we give, not simply who we are."

Keischa felt her chest tighten. That definitely mirrored her thoughts and actions. Simone's words sounded like they could have come straight out of her own mouth.

Traci validated her thoughts as she continued, "You are not alone. These wounds echo over and over. They show up where you over-give, where you never feel like enough is enough at work, or with partners. Where you chase the need for love and affection even when you know it's not there, and that you aren't safe to be you. Attachment wounds are not flaws, they're a blueprint we learned. But here's what I want you all to take note of, write it in your notebook, put a star on it as important, highlight it, whatever it takes: Blueprints can be revised."

As Keischa was writing this fact and circling it, her mind flashed to Malcolm. *"Hmm,"* Keischa thought. Malcolm had become part of her blueprint without her fully recognizing it. He had shown her that he carried resentment from past relationships and doubted real connection existed. He questioned Keischa's use of her time. He accused her of being unavailable to meet his needs. He disappeared for days, only to resurface with apologies saying he had needed space and peace. The issue wasn't just him, being him. It was also her wound whispering, *"You need to show up bigger, you need to make him see you're valuable. Love harder, or he will leave. People leave."* Keischa was finally feeling the weight of the cycle and realizing where she had let things slide because she wanted to keep the peace. She was realizing how she felt about their relationship wasn't up to Malcolm. She was changing herself to accommodate him.

Her thoughts were drawn back to the group as she heard Traci saying, "Attachment wounds show up when the love we needed most wasn't consistent, safe, or nurturing. For many of us Black women, it wasn't just personal. It was generational. We learned to survive instead of thrive. We learned strength, but not softness. And those wounds don't disappear, unfortunately, they replay in our relationships." She paused, scanning the room.

"Think about it. How many of you have chased love that couldn't hold you? Or stayed silent because you were afraid speaking up meant being left?" Hands went up. Keischa's included.

"That's not a personality flaw. That's an attachment wound," Traci continued. "Once, I begged a man to stay. Even when every part of me knew he wasn't choosing, or would never choose, me. I slowly began to realize, there was an echo of a childhood where most times my needs felt invisible. Here's the tea, therapy helped me stop betraying myself for the sake of being chosen, and start seeing myself as valuable enough for someone to finally see me." Keischa felt the words slice through her. She saw Malcolm's inconsistency, Simone's sharpness, and her own exhaustion reflected back. For the first time, she didn't feel alone.

Traci The Therapist

The Thursday afternoon before Keischa's first session, Traci prepared her notes and allowed herself a moment to reflect on her own beginning of accepting help and healing. She remembered the night she finally broke. At twenty-four, sitting on the floor of her one-bedroom apartment surrounded by unopened bills, a failed relationship, and empty wine bottles she was falling apart. In tears, feeling heavy and alone her mother's voice replayed in her head, sharp and dismissive, "You think anybody's gonna love you if you keep crying like that? Get up and figure it out. You always whining or crying."

She'd been in a relationship with a man who mirrored her mother's coldness, who withheld affection like punishment. She caught herself begging him, screaming at him in an often-replayed argument, "Please, can you just see me? Listen to me! Pay attention!" In that moment, she realized she was reenacting her childhood wound.

That was her breaking point. That was the night she vowed to not only heal herself, but to help other women break free from those cycles. Therapy wasn't just a career. It was redemption. Now, years later, she would soon be sitting across from Keischa, ready to guide her through the same journey.

Today was Keischa's first individual therapy session with Traci. And though she had been to workshops and group settings before, this felt different. Intimate. Personal. She lingered in the reception area, willing herself to check-in. She wondered if she was truly ready to face herself. Keischa was snapped back to reality by a gentle hand on her shoulder.

"Ms. Keischa," the receptionist said with a gentleness that caught her off guard. She wasn't used to the soft tone and kindness. "Ms. Traci is ready to see you."

When Keischa finally sat across from Traci in the therapy office, her hands trembled. The space was warm, filled with soft colors, and gentle lighting. It was nothing like she expected. No clipboard tapping. No cold stares. Just Traci, leaning forward, eyes soft with curiosity. For a moment, Keischa considered bolting. But something in Traci's presence, as usual, was steady and calm, it was enough to keep her seated.

"I've never done this before," she admitted.

Traci smiled gently. "That's okay. You're here, and that's the first step."

Keischa looked down. "I don't even know where to start. I just know I'm tired. Tired of fixing, tired of being strong, tired of men who say they'll stay and don't. Tired of giving and still feeling empty. I'm scared people will leave me."

Traci leaned in. "What you're describing isn't weakness. It's survival fatigue. You've been carrying wounds that were never yours to carry. What if we start with the understanding that therapy isn't about fixing you, but helping you lay some of that weight down?"

Tears welled up before Keischa could stop them. For the first time she heard her own voice admit out loud, "I don't even know who I'd be without the weight."

"Then that's where we start," Traci continued. "You've been carrying so much alone. Therapy is the place where you don't have to. This is your space to heal those wounds, not erase them, but transform them." Then she said something that let Keischa feel as though she could breathe. "Let's find out who you are without those weights together." For many people, that phrase sounds gentle. For Keischa, it was revolutionary. For the first time in years, Keischa felt a flicker of hope.

Interventions for Healing Attachment Wounds

1. The Vulnerability Letter (Revised)

•   Write a letter to someone you trust sharing something you normally hide.

•   Notice how your body feels as you write.

•   Send it only if you feel safe. Or keep it as proof that you can voice your truth.

2. Maslow Ladder Reflection

•   Draw the pyramid. Identify where you feel stuck.

•   Write what you need at that level. Do you need Safety? Belonging? Esteem?

•   Write one step you can take this week toward fulfilling it.

3. Attachment Wound Body Scan

•   Sit quietly and think of a relationship trigger.

•   Notice where the pain sits in your body (chest, stomach, jaw).

•   Place your hand there and repeat, "I am safe. I am seen. I am loved."

4. Safe Relationship Blueprint

•   Create a list of non-negotiables that make you feel secure.

•   Next time you date or build a friendship, compare behaviors to this blueprint.

- If they can't meet your security baseline, they can't meet you.

Affirmations

- I am not defined by my wounds.
- I can learn new ways of loving and being loved.
- My past does not dictate my future.
- I am worthy of steady, secure, unconditional love.

Scripture for Reflection

"The Lord is close to the brokenhearted and saves those who are crushed in spirit." — Psalm 34:18

Chapter Nine

Rest as Resistance

"Rest is not a luxury for Black women: it's an act of defiance."
– Tricia Hersey (The Nap Bishop)

Keischa

Keischa had been pacing around the living room, rethinking her decision to have Simone come over and kick it. They had developed a good "friendship" if that was the right word. She had been taught not to use the "F" word too loosely. People had to earn friendship. Everybody wasn't your friend. Keischa knew to put people in the associate category until they proved themselves. She had been told over and over again, "You can't trust everybody. They will turn on you." Problem was, nobody ever taught her how to make "friends" and what the criteria was for this earned right.

She stood there loving and admiring her space and the smell. The smell was so calming to her, intoxicating. Not the sweet vanilla stuff people tended to gear toward. She was more of an earthy girl. The candles she was vibing with today were in a beautiful muted black holder, her signature candle scent was amber and tobacco with a wooden wick. The crackling sound of that wick just felt like comfort and peace.

She remembered how her thumb had hovered over her phone debating if she should hit send. She reread the text she'd sent to Simone earlier that morning, the one that had made her stomach twist, "Hey, I owe you a date. You can come by tonight if you want. I'll make food. No pressure."

It was short and clumsy, but honest. It was her way of saying "I miss you" without saying it. Vulnerability still made her uncomfortable, but something inside her had shifted. After that last workshop with Traci, she had decided she was tired of being the version of herself that only operated on emotional autopilot. It was a simple message, but it felt like exposure. It felt like a naked confession that she wanted connection. And when Simone replied, "Yup, girl, I'd love that," her heart fluttered in a way she hadn't felt in a long time.

Simone

Simone sat in her car and reread the text message she got from Keischa earlier. Her thoughts, as usual, were spiraling. She had answered quickly and now was rethinking her answer. She had never been a girl's girl or a bestie. Other women always seemed to misunderstand her or expect so much from her. Simone never felt like she could rest or relax in friendships, so she always over-gave, overperformed, and over-cared.

Resenting these unreciprocal relationships, she began showing up as mean, sarcastic, hard, and guarded. Simone felt the tug of pain remembering how she was the household anchor. When her dad left and her mom had to work more hours, she became the caregiver and the person who needed to secure the needs of others.

In this moment, she felt in danger of being hurt again. She never prioritized herself and it had caused her pain. This relationship with Keisch felt different, and she didn't want to ruin it with her insecurities and trauma. Sooo, she texted back "yes", quickly before she could change her mind. Now, here she was. Heart pounding, holding her breath, knocking on Keischa's door.

Keischa

Keischa took a deep breath, glanced around at the soft light spilling from the floor lamp, and admired the carefully prepared charcuterie board she had learned to make from watching YouTube videos. She was loving the beautiful way she had laid it out on the table, and the two fluted glasses of strawberry basil mocktails (nothing she would usually drink, but she was keeping it cute). The music was upbeat and happy. It had taken her an hour to convince herself that letting Simone come over wasn't a mistake, so she wanted to make sure everything was perfect.

She was startled out of her thoughts by Simone's knock. Keischa opened the door to find her friend standing there in jeans and an oversized hoodie, her face was a mixture of curiosity and hesitation. She really looked beautiful.

"Girl, you look good," Keischa said smiling, feeling happy she had extended the invitation. Simone smiled, that half-smile that could mean a thousand things. It was a familiar smile. Then, she burst out laughing saying, "Girl, I almost didn't come. I was scared, not of you, but of feeling close to someone again."

Keischa nodded, eyes glassy but calm. "I get it. I almost didn't send the text. I sat there staring at it for ten minutes. My chest felt tight.' Keischa wanted to say that vulnerability felt like that sometimes, it was like waiting for a rejection that may never come, but decided to keep that tidbit to herself. Instead, she said, "Yeah, I almost didn't invite you, for the exact same reason," They laughed, heartily and genuinely. The laughter felt good.

Once inside, Simone sat at the edge of the couch draped in a soft throw, she sat quietly stirring her mocktail. She glanced around the room, noticing the way every corner was intentionally soft. The framed photo of Keischa's kids, a worn Bible on the table, and affirmations written on sticky notes by the mirror. "You've got peace in here, huh?" Simone muttered.

Keischa smiled and perked up. "Yeah, girl," she said sweetly, "If I can't get it out there, in the streets. Imma create it here on the inside. But girl, this the easy part. The hard part is working on relationships that allow vulnerability, trust, and the ability to rest without feeling like I gotta perform or pretend. Anywho ma'am, I'm really glad you here and we are getting close."

Simone giggled, "Ok girl, now it's still early. Dont be getting all mushy on me. Whatcha wanna do? Netflix, Uno Karoke... You name it. I'm game."

Keischa stared at Simone, she was such a free spirit. She watched her as she sat absent mindedly munching on chocolate covered pretzels and sipping her mocktail. *"I wish I was more like Simone,"* she thought. *"She can say anything, even the hard things, and not filter herself. She is just real."*

Yup, that's why she was drawn to her. She was... what's the word? Yeah, unapologetic. Keischa wondered what living in that world felt like. Keischa was more tender, performative, and needy. Simone was looking at her quizzically. "Earth to Keisch. Earth to Keischa. Girl, where you go?" she said laughing in her comfortable way.

"I'm here," Keischa said. "Girl, I'm here. And for the first time, I feel safe. Let's put a lil' something in these mocktails and door dash some hot wings. I got the UNO cards ready. Get ready to catch this beat down!"

The Workshop: Rest as a Love Language

The workshop was a place of comfort, energy, and quiet love for Keischa. The smell, the familiarity, and the women who came together in a Black girl type of solidarity. The room was already filling up by the time Keischa and Simone arrived at the next workshop. The air buzzed with quiet energy and anticipation of what was to come. The kind of energy that comes when a room full of Black women show up to talk about things they were told not to talk about.

Traci stood at the front in a flowy mustard colored jumpsuit, hair in soft curls, eyes bright but steady. Keischa loved how she was the authority in the room, but felt like she was one of them living the same life experiences and helping to heal. Traci made her feel safe, vulnerable, and seen just by being there. Today, though, something in her demeanor felt different, softer, maybe a little heavier.

"Let's talk about rest," she began. "Not sleeping in, not laziness, but a basic human need. The kind of rest that changes the nervous system. She walked to the board, "Y'all already knew I was going to take it back to our friend, Maslow." She drew Maslow's pyramid with a thick black marker, "Physiological Needs, Safety, Love and Belonging, Esteem, and our girl, Self-actualization." She circled the bottom two rungs.

"Rest," she started slowly, as the ladies leaned in pens poised to take notes, "sits under Physiological Needs and Safety. It's foundational. If you aren't resting, your body's basic needs aren't met, which means your nervous system is stuck in alarm status. You can't properly access love, esteem, or purpose when you live in chronic depletion."

The room stirred. Someone sighed. Heads nodded. Someone whispered, "Amen."

"And when we talk about our attachment," Traci continued much softer, "rest is relational. Your attachment style determines whether you believe rest is safe. Some of us were raised to think rest equals weakness. Some equate rest with abandonment. For some, rest triggers anxiety because stillness lets old pain catch up."

That hit some of the ladies with revelation. A woman wiped her eyes, Keischa's throat tightened, and she noticed Simone had her arms folded tightly across her chest intensely staring at Traci.

Traci walked about the circle and talked, "For some of us, we never learned to rest because we were too busy surviving." Traci paused, looked at the women and continued, "For Black women, rest has always been rebellion. We come from generations of women who never stopped moving, not because they didn't want to, but because they couldn't. My grandmother used to say, 'If I sit down too long, something gon' fall apart.' And that stayed in me. Maybe it stayed in you too."

She paused and let that settle. Traci inhaled slowly. She looked calm, poised, and anchored. She was teaching Black women how to unlearn the lie that they didn't need rest or to slow down, that they weren't human. But inside the topic was hitting her like a bruise that was being pressed way too hard. The memory of sitting outside of her second job, hands shaking and her eye twitching, flooded her thoughts.

In those days, she hadn't slept well. Really, not at all. Her mind was constantly on that God-awful to do list. Children at home to take care of, a partner who rarely showed up, and a mother who had all the answers but none of the support. The words from her mother kept playing in her head, "A tired Black woman is a productive one." As if exhaustion was a sign of dignity.

Traci learned early: If I stop, everything falls apart. She had been taught that rest equaled shame. In order to unlearn that mantra, she started going a little slower, a little quieter, taking small steps until she learned that rest wasn't a withdrawal from responsibility– it was an act of stewardship and love over herself. Traci pulled herself back into the room of listening women.

"I was thirty-three when I ended up in the emergency room," she said. "Heart pounding so hard I thought I was dying. I was working two jobs, taking care of the family and home, as well as helping my mama with her meds. I was talking my friends down from emotional ledges and showing up for everybody but me. The doctor said it was exhaustion. I WAS exhausted. My body was screaming for what my spirit kept refusing. REST. Rest is not indulgence. Rest is necessary. Rest is self-love." The room was quiet.

"I realized that I'd been living in survival mode, stuck on the bottom rung of Maslow's hierarchy. I kept performing to prove my worth. Even therapy was a performance at first. But rest? Rest forced me to confront who I was when I wasn't proving something."

Simone nodded slowly. Keischa felt her own chest tighten again and her breathing deepened.

Traci looked around. "Rest threatens that. Because rest says: "You are already enough." A murmur rippled through the room. Traci smiled gently. "No pressure, as always, but is there anyone who would like to share what rest means to them?"

Simone raised her hand, surprising herself. She heard her voice crack as Traci asked her, "What's coming up for you?" she added, "Remember, you are in a safe space for honest reflection."

"Honestly," she spoke in a small voice, "I don't rest because if I stop spinning the plates, if I stop moving, people stop needing me. Who am I, if I'm not needed?" Simone broke down sobbing. There it was out there in the air, raw, spoken unvarnished truth. She swallowed hard but continued. "My entire life has been 'Simone is so dependable. Girl, you are the strongest person I know.' I'm the fixer, with people talking to me for hours about how to fix some part of their emotional devastation. I'm the one who shows up. Everyone's go-to, no consideration for just me. I'm always number one on the list for what people need. So, if I change this... if I can change this, I don't even know who I would be."

Traci, compassionately placed her hand on Simones's shoulder and asked, "Where do you feel that emotion in your body?"

Simone closed her eyes. "My chest, right in the middle, feels heavy like something is laying on me." Simone opened her eyes, surprised.

Traci stepped forward. "That's emotional labor sitting in your chest. That's years of hyper-independence and anxious-avoidant attachment. It's you wearing the familiar mask of hiding behind 'I got it', or 'I can do it myself.' That's you not yet knowing that you don't earn love through giving all of you to prove you are worthy or needed. Rest is honoring the fact that you can't keep giving to exhaustion. Rest is learning how to give yourself love."

Simone listened, soaking in every word and marveled at how light she suddenly felt. Keischa nervously spoke next. "For me, rest feels unsafe. Like if I stop, I'll lose everything that I worked hard for and everyone that I need." Her voice cracked.

Traci stepped closer. "That's the attachment wound talking," she said softly. "The part of you that learned love is earned by doing, not by being. Now," she said in a loud and happy voice, "with that, let's all get into the work."

Later, after the workshop, women gathered around Traci with questions, reflections, and the need to connect further. Keischa and Simone lingered too, sensing that the story wasn't over.

"I think a lot about my mother," Traci said, eyes soft. "I watched my mother work herself to the bone and make herself sick. I watched her body quit before she did. I swore I'd never be that woman and then I became her in a different form. Overachieving, always saying yes, always saving, neglecting my needs, and betraying myself. It took years of therapy to realize I was addicted to being needed. My rest felt like betrayal."

Her voice trembled. "That's the honest note. Healing isn't pretty. Sometimes it's sitting on the floor surrounded by the wreckage of who you thought you had to be. But the good thing is that's where you start to rebuild."

Simone wiped her eyes. Keischa's heart pounded. That story, the rawness of it, the vulnerability hit something inside of them and created a space for self-honesty and readiness.

The Therapy Session

A few days later, Keischa sat in the soft beige chair of Traci's office. A box of tissues sat within reach. The room smelled faintly of eucalyptus. It was warm and inviting, she let her shoulders relax. Keischa giggled to herself as she lay back on the big comfy couch. Pictures and narratives of being on the couch for therapy were suddenly funny to her.

"So," Traci said gently. "How was the last workshop for you?"

Keischa laughed, short and shaky. "The same as the others, triggering, beautiful, connected, and necessary. All the things."

Traci smiled. "Yes, that's usually how it goes. There was a lot that was covered. What was something that made you think about your life? We are connecting the dots to see where you might be stuck."

Silence settled for a moment before Keischa spoke again. "I realized something. I'm not always sure if I can trust my emotions or if my perception of things is right. With Malcolm, you remember him. He's always hot or cold, the problem with that is it's always unsettling. I never know what I'm going to get or when I'm going to get it. I think I'm in a romantic relationship, but maybe that's in my mind. The relationship with Simone seems easy and is growing, but I don't want to move too fast and realize that the relationship was built up in my head. The real issue, I believe, is I can't trust the relationship I have with myself. I feel like I betray myself to make relationships work."

"Tell me more about what you saw or felt about resting and trusting yourself in your childhood," Traci said, leaning in.

Keischa closed her eyes and started slowly. "When I was young, my mom worked nights. I had to take care of my siblings. Looking back, I don't believe I felt like there was space for me to be tired, for me to be wrong. And if I ever felt like I was overwhelmed, my mom would say, 'Thank you, Keisch. I couldn't do this without you. You are helping keep this family together. We need to work together.' I watched my mother wait for a man who never came. But that wouldn't stop her from waiting for him. When he would show up, she would light up like Christmas morning. Love arrived inconsistent, if at all. I learned..." Keischa said, full of shame and guilt, "to trust cautiously, to want selectively, and to over function to secure safety. Rest and love, whatever they were, were dangerous.

Keischa stared at her hands. Then continued, "With Malcolm, I pretend that he's complicated. He isn't. I use that as an excuse to stay. He's good at whatever minimum he gives me whenever he's present. But he disappears emotionally, especially at the times I need him the most. And every time he does, I chase him. I say I want peace, but I run toward chaos because it feels familiar. Truthfully, safe."

Traci nodded slowly. "That's the anxious-avoidant dance. You crave connection, but he fears it. And both of you are repeating something you learned long before you met."

"Attachment wounds," Keischa whispered.

"Yes," Traci nodded. "That's what attachment wounds do. They make rest impossible because rest requires vulnerability. It means letting someone see you unguarded. And the wounds reopen when we're trying to love, pretending we are getting our needs met. You equate your needs to inconvenience. Rest is the bridge to emotional safety. Without rest, your attachment system stays activated, as we talked about. Then your relationships feel threatening instead of nourishing."

Keischa's mind was reeling. She whispered, "So, Traci, real talk. Do I sabotage rest AND love?"

"Not sabotage," Traci corrected. "Protect. You're protecting the little girl inside you who never felt safe enough to stop moving. Rest becomes thought of as a luxury, something you have to earn or deserve." Keischa's mind drifted to Malcolm and how this was starting to make sense.

Malcolm

Malcolm sat in his car outside his ex's house, waiting to pick up his daughter, Mari. The porch light flickered, and for a second, he saw the reflection of his father in his rearview mirror. He had a strong jaw, was handsome, charismatic, and brewing in silent anger, dysfunction, and chaos.

He remembered his father and mother yelling at each other, hushed phone conversations, his mother constantly in tears. His father would leave on weekends, saying, "I need space," but never explaining what that meant. As a kid, Malcolm had promised he wouldn't be that man. And yet, here he was, thirty-six and repeating the same patterns in every relationship he tried to hold on to.

He thought about Keischa and the way she looked at him like she saw the good in him, his potential. It scared him, but he longed for it to continue, so he fed into her emotional insecurity by making promises he wasn't prepared to keep. Because if he kept her believing in him, and the promise of the fairytale ending, she wouldn't leave. Yet, he would leave emotionally, then physically over and over. He would come back because of the emotional and physical security she provided. It was the love he grew up with, the familiar love he knew and craved.

"Daddy!" Mari's voice cut through his thoughts. He turned, smiled. She was his soft place, his do-over. He took her hand, vowing again to be better.

Simone

Simone stood in her kitchen late that night, washing dishes. The workshop had stirred so many emotions in her. Pain, anger, and relief all tangled up.

She thought of her mother, a woman who never rested either. Always cleaning, always hosting, always "doing." The only time Simone had seen her mother rest was in her casket. That image had burned into her mind, the stillness of death mistaken for peace.

No wonder she was afraid to stop moving. She thought about her attachment system. Hyper alert, anxious, wary of closeness, protective of her space. She learned rest wasn't optional, it was dangerous. Rest for Simone wasn't a pause, it was a risk.

Her phone buzzing startled her. It was a text from Keischa. "You good? Girl, I'm still thinking about this concept of rest."

Simone typed, paused, deleted, then finally sent, "Yeah. I know I'm still processing lol. I love you, thanks for checking in." After she hit the send button, she thought, *"Girl, why did you do that? Why didn't you say, 'You free? Let's talk. It's a lot going through my mind.' Hmmm."*

The Workshop's Aftermath

The following week, the workshop theme was "Redirection: Choosing New Narratives." Traci stood in front of the group again, but this time, her tone was lighter. "When we rest, we create room to rewrite our stories. We start moving up Maslow's ladder, from survival to belonging, from belonging to esteem, and from esteem to self-actualization."

She smiled at Keischa. "Self-actualization isn't a destination. It's a daily decision to live as your whole self, not your wounded one."

Simone raised her hand. "So... what happens when you rest and the world doesn't?"

Traci smiled. "You rest anyway. That's resistance. There's a quote in a scene from the sitcom "Good Times", yes, I know I'm dating myself, where the character Thelma and her husband Keith are arguing because he is feeling his value and self-worth are gone because he can no longer play pro football. Thelma tells him, 'The world is going to go on whether you are sitting on top of it or stretched out under it.'"

The women nodded, some with tears in their eyes.

Keischa's Letter

That night, at home, Keischa sat at her desk with a blank page in front of her. Traci had assigned an exercise, a Vulnerability Letter. She took a breath and began to write:

"Dear Self,

I'm learning to sit still without guilt. To breathe without apologizing. Rest used to feel like weakness, but now I see it is strength.
I forgive you for running. I forgive you for mistaking exhaustion for love. You don't have to prove you're worthy anymore. You just are."

She folded the letter, slid it into her journal, and smiled for the first time in days.

Keischa woke the next morning to sunlight spilling across her face. The world felt quieter, softer. She reached for her phone, as she usually did early in the morning, a habit she had been trying to change, and two messages waited.

One from Simone, "Hey, girlie, what up? Coffee later?"

And from Malcolm, "Thinking about you. What's up with you? Missing you."

She smiled faintly and put the phone back down. She didn't rush to respond. She stretched, exhaled, and whispered into the quiet, "I'm resting. New phone, who dis???"

Tools For The Reader

1. The Rest Ritual

Choose one evening a week to disconnect, no phone, no noise, no productivity.   Prepare your space with intention: candle, music, tea, silence. Tell yourself, "I am safe to be still." Rest is not avoidance, it's recovery.

2. The Attachment Reflection Exercise

Ask yourself: What did I learn about love from watching adults in my life?

- Did they rest?
- Did they nurture themselves?
- What beliefs about rest and worth did I inherit — and which ones do I want to unlearn?

3. Redirection Practice

Every time you feel the pull to overextend, pause and ask: "Am I doing this from love or fear?" Redirect one small action each day toward peace instead of performance.

4. Boundaries for Rest

Rest doesn't mean accessibility. Tell loved ones, "I'll get back to you after I rest." Protecting your peace is sacred work.

Affirmations for Rest

- I am not lazy for resting. I am healing.
- My worth is not tied to my output.
- My peace is my birthright.
- I am learning to rest without guilt, without fear, without apology.

- I am becoming the version of me that feels safe to exhale.

Scripture for Reflection

"Come to me, all you who are weary and burdened, and I will give you rest." — Matthew 11:28

Chapter Ten

The Importance of Boundaries

"A boundary is an act of self-love disguised as protection." –
Shaaree McCalpine

Keischa

Keischa stood in the doorway of her bedroom, staring at her phone as if
it had personally betrayed her. Malcolm had sent his familiar routine text
saying, "Thinking about you... missing you." It still sat on the lock screen
like a touch she hadn't asked for. This text tugged at her chest. It was the
pull she always felt when he reached out after ghosting her. This time last
year she would have been joyful, grateful, living in a fallacy that this was
love. She giggled to herself, "Dang them workshops and therapy sessions,"
she said out loud. *"I'm definitely growing and I'm loving the process,"* she
thought. Bursting out laughing, she reveled in how she was changing into
a version of herself that allowed her to consider herself first.

The old version of her would have texted back before the message
even had time to breathe.But this morning, she didn't. Something in her
whispered, *"Not today."* She realized that therapy had given her the tools
to understand that spiraling about Malcolm's disappearances and silences
had been part of her routine and attachment style. Understanding patterns
in herself, and the why behind them, had changed so much. Resting in
abandonment was no longer part of her safety plan.

Her thoughts were interrupted by Haven and Devin laughing and grabbing her legs, "Mom, the timer went off. Remember? You said when that happens", they started signing out, "Weeeee gotta go."

"Yes," she said, "thanks for the reminder, loves. Let's get outta here." It warmed her heart that learning to rest had replaced chaotic mornings with routine and smiles for her and the kids. In the workshop, Traci had taught that chaos is internal and if we let it go unchecked it becomes our normal routine. Keischa thought to herself, *"I get to create the routine and decide if it's chaotic or restful."*

Rest, as Traci taught, had opened something in her. A quiet clarity. A shift in her awareness. And now, as she looked into the kids' eager faces, she wasn't annoyed. She wasn't overwhelmed. She was ready. She felt, in real time, closeness and consistency. Her presence was appreciated and she wasn't on autopilot. She felt accountability for her life. She finally understood that love could show up as safety.

Keischa's phone buzzed with Simone 's text, "Girl!!! Traci said the next workshop is boundaries. You READY??"

Simone was always so enthusiastic and, ironically, right on time. Was this girl living in her head right now? She texted back, " Yeah, girl! I literally was just thinking about boundaries. I'm definitely ready. See you soon."

The text made her realize that she wanted more, deserved more, from Malcolm, from others, and from herself. Getting more required boundaries. Yep, she was reading for the workshop.

Just as she went to set her phone down, her nervous system was ramped up by a text that came through, "Hey girlie, I'm in town and can't wait to see you."

This girl had rocked Keischa's peace for years. The text was from her older cousin. Her first teacher of unhealthy loyalty. Her earliest blueprint for blurred boundaries, Rayna.

That name took her back to her fourteen-year-old self. The smell of the flat iron plugged in and burnt hair oil fills the cramped bedroom as Rayna sits on the floor, legs stretched out, painting her toes a bright bold purple.

"Keisch, go get my purse," she says without looking up. Keischa doesn't move. She was sitting on the bed with her workbook, trying to finish math homework before school the next day.

"I'm doing homework," she whispered.

Rayna snapped her neck around so fast her hoop earrings swung. "And? You acting brand new. Who you talking to? Girl, go get my purse." She went. She always went.

And when Rayna needed money, she asked Keischa to borrow some, knowing damn well she wouldn't pay it back. When she needed someone to lie to Mama, she'd guilt-trip her to do it. When she needed anything: clothes, babysitting, someone to be an emotional dumping space, someone to lean on for emotional security, Keischa was the designated fallback girl. Not because she wanted to be, but because her childhood had taught her that family meant obligation. And obligation meant loyalty. It meant survival. Keischa caught her breath as the memory faded.

God, even after all these years Rayna still lived in her nervous system and her memories. Keischa now understood what Traci meant when she talked about relationships in her last therapy session. She had said, "Unhealed relationships don't disappear. They calcify into belief systems." That statement was hitting hard today. She deleted the text, wrote a reminder to herself to discuss this in her next session, and got back to her day.

Simone

Simone sat at her kitchen table, staring into a cold cup of coffee she had reheated three times and still hadn't drunk. She had tons of work to do, but just couldn't get motivated to start. She had texted Keischa about the workshop and she was eager to get to it. These workshops had given her so much peace, change, and even though she used to hate the word (because it seemed like a buzzword), empowerment. Boundaries were stirring in her spirit. She wanted to learn more about how to set them because today they felt more like confusion than clarity.

Her phone was lit up signaling a notification. It was her mom. Again. Even though she fully understood that she would be working.

"Hey baby, I need you to come help me move these boxes. My back is acting up. You know I can't do this stuff on my own."

The familiar dread dropped in her stomach like a stone. The dread that came from being the designated strong one, the reliable one, the one who never said no even when her soul begged her to. She typed, "Okay, I'll be there in an hour."

But her thumb hovered and for the first time she hesitated. She thought about the previous workshop. The moment she cried in front of all those women. The feeling of freedom. The freedom to choose herself instead of doing something for the sake of doing or obligation. The feeling of something loosening in her chest. Something like freedom trying to crawl out. She reread her text and decided to delete it.

Instead, she typed, "Mom, I can't come today. I'm working." Her heart raced. Her palms sweated. Her body screamed, "Girl, what did you just do?!" Her mind repeated what people had always told her anytime she had a negative opinion of her mom, "You only get one mother. She needs you."

But under that panic was something softer. Something new. Something sacred. A boundary. She looked at the phone, took a deep breath, and whispered to herself,
"I deserve to not be needed all the time." And hit send.

The Workshop: Boundaries as Self-Love, better yet, Self-Like

The room was already buzzing when Keischa and Simone arrived. Black women filled the space with the kind of quiet resilience that comes from surviving things nobody talked about or apologized for. Traci stood in front of the group in a copper-toned dress, hair pulled back, face glowing with peace and confidence.

"All right ladies," she began, warmth coating her voice. "Welcome, y'all. Tonight we will talk about boundaries."

A low murmur rippled through the room.

Ok, loves. It's me again, your author friend. I want to take a brief pause before we get back to Traci and her workshop. Let's love on ourselves for a minute. Hold, hug, and embrace yourself. Breathe in. 1, 2, 3 breathe out. Breathe again. And now relax.

Let's take a moment to Hokey Pokey out our tension. Turn yourself around, shake it out, and that's what it's all about hockey pokey! I'm sure you have a smile on your face at this point, or are even laughing out loud. And that is really the point, letting yourself relax, laugh, and breathe. Now back to the workshop.

Traci started speaking with authority, "Black women weren't taught boundaries, we were taught roles: teacher, fixer, healer, mother, counselor, backbone, therapist, maid, prayer warrior, emotional mule. We were taught to absorb everything and complain about nothing."

A collective, "Mmm-hmm," echoed sharp and knowing.

Traci went to the whiteboard. Everyone eagerly pulled out notebooks and phones ready for the juicy details. She began to draw her familiar pyramid on the whiteboard. The group laughed as we all said in unison, "Our friend, Maslow."

"Yup", Traci chucked. "You got it. Let's bring back our friend, Maslow." She wrote: Safety. Love & Belonging. Esteem.

"Boundaries," she said, "live right between safety and belonging. Without them, you can't climb the pyramid. You can't feel safe, because people's demands keep violating your peace. Let me repeat that. YOU can't feel safe, because people's demands keep violating your peace. And you can't feel belonging, because you're too busy performing and pretending."

Simone felt the words hit. This related to the exact situation she had been in this morning.

"And attachment?" Traci continued. "Oh, boundaries reveal your attachment style QUICK." She counted on her fingers. "One, if you're anxiously attached, boundaries feel like abandonment. Two, if you're avoidant, they feel suffocating. Three, if you're disorganized, boundaries feel like a threat AND a relief." Keischa shifted in her seat.

Traci's eyes softened as she scanned the room, "When we didn't have boundaries as children, we learned that love is something we protect by over-giving. We learned to keep the peace, even if it costs us our identity. Listen to me carefully. Boundaries don't push people away. They reveal who is willing to come closer with respect."

The room went silent. A few women asked to share and revealed how this lesson made sense in how they show up in their relationships. Traci looked around the room giving everyone the space to feel connected and safe. When her gaze landed on Keischa, she felt Traci's loving understanding that had become a place of safety and welcome for her. She also felt the tears falling down her cheek as she slowly raised her hand.

"Keisch," Traci said in her gentle warm tone, "what's coming up for you?" Keischa swallowed hard. "Boundaries feel dangerous," she whispered. "Like saying 'no' means I'll lose people. Like I have to accept whatever someone gives me. I feel like I put too much emphasis on a man, Malcolm. He takes up too much space, in my thoughts, out loud in my conversations, and in my mind trying to figure out where I stand. Especially when he becomes silent, distant, and invisible." A few heads nodded in recognition.

Traci stepped closer. "That's the part of you that learned as a girl that love is earned, not given. That your needs inconvenience people. That advocating for yourself creates conflict." Keischa blinked. It felt like Traci was reading the chapters of her childhood out loud.

"And the girl who learned those lessons grew into a woman who doesn't protect herself," Traci said softly. "But you're not that little girl anymore." Something inside Keischa felt like she knew this, but had not allowed herself the luxury of addressing it.

"What if I lose him?" she asked, voice trembling.

Traci smiled. "Here's the thing," she began softly. "If you create a boundary and it makes you lose someone, they never planned to respect you, change, or consider your feelings to begin with. This is where we settle into the sections of the pyramid that give us safety, love, and belonging and continue to build our esteem." Traci looked up and said to all of us, "All, this work is an inside job."

She continued writing on the board: LOVE LANGUAGES x MASLOW x ATTACHMENT. "How many have heard of the popular love languages?" she asked. Hands flew up, as women were blurting out what their love language was based on the quiz they had taken. She turned to face the women. "Remember, your love language is not what makes you romantic. It's the words that tell you where you were wounded."

The room grew silent. Traci continued writing, and said into the board, "I think I heard someone say: Acts of service. Who feels loved when someone helps you carry the load?"

Hands went up. There was a lot of agreement and "girl, yeses". Simone's hand was halfway up, like she didn't want to be seen, but needed to be seen at the same time.

"For many Black women," Traci continued, "Acts of Service aren't cute gestures. They answer a need and deeper questions like: Does this act help me feel safe? Does this help me, so I get to rest? That's Maslow's hierarchy showing up as safety needs. It's the way someone proves they won't abandon responsibility."

Heads nodded. "That's me," someone whispered.

"Anyone say Quality Time?" Traci went on pointing to the next love language she had written on the board. "If you grew up with an inconsistent presence, you might cling to time with someone like oxygen. That's the belonging piece. Attachment patterns show up amidst insecurity and get louder when you don't feel the security of having consistency. It's the ache of emotional neglect." Keisch exhaled slowly. Yep, that part.

"Words of Affirmation, anyone?" Traci said. "That mirrors Maslow's Esteem level: the need for validation. For some of us, no matter how many degrees or accomplishments we earn, if we don't hear 'I'm proud of you' or are celebrated it hits like we're still that little girl waiting on praise that never came. It's the voice you didn't get growing up."

"Gifts? That's reassurance of worth. Especially, for those who grew up being told they were 'too much' or 'not enough.' And Physical Touch? That's safety and presence. That's wanting to be held by someone who doesn't turn cold."

Keischa noticed an older deeply melanated woman, whose face looked aged and a lil tired ,but beautiful none the less across the room. She had dimples that peeked through her cheeks and softened her expression before any words could come out of her mouth. She placed her hand over her heart. That gesture demonstrated a knowing that came with hurt and experience. It looked like she was validated with this one.

"Here's the thing," Traci said, lowering her voice. "Our love languages reveal our unmet needs. Boundaries protect those needs once we finally name them."

The room breathed out as one. The group sat silent for a moment. Then Traci asked if anyone was willing to share.

"I set a boundary with my Mom today," Simone said softly, hands twisting in her lap. "I told her I couldn't help. I felt selfish. It was hard, but it also felt freeing." The women hummed approvingly.

"It felt like I was choosing myself," she continued. "Which is new for me. It felt scary. Real scary. I didn't want to disappoint her or make her mad."

Traci nodded. "That's because boundaries activate your attachment wounds before they heal them." A beat passed. Then she added,"Boundaries require you to believe you're worth protecting. And that's the real work."

Simone exhaled through her nose,"Whew Chile. Yeah, you said it."

Traci clasped her hands, "Let's do a quick exercise." She handed out a sheet titled The Boundary Quiz. Traci took one and passed down the rest of the small half-sheets.

"At the top, under the heading it says 'The Boundary Blueprint,'" she explained. "Circle what hits for you. No one sees this unless you want them to."

Keischa stared at the page and circled more than she left blank. Her throat tightened on the last one.

The Boundary Blueprint:

- I say 'yes' when I mean 'no'.
- I over-explain my 'no'.
- I accept inconsistency because I'm scared to be alone.
- I confuse being needed with being loved.
- I feel guilty when I rest.
- I make myself small to keep the peace.
- I shrink my needs because someone else might be inconvenienced.
- I give open access to people who drain me.
- I often confuse chaos with chemistry.
- I forgive people who continue the same patterns and behaviors they say they will change.

Simone circled 'I confuse being needed with being loved' so hard the pen almost tore the paper.

Traci continued, "Boundaries are not punishment. Boundaries are clarity. Let's clarify the difference. A boundary is about self-protection and self-regulation. It answers 'What will I do to take care of myself?' Boundaries are rooted in safety, values, and emotional regulation. They teach people how to love you. And they teach you who can't."

"We don't want to confuse boundaries with punishment. Pay attention when your boundary sounds like control, retaliation, or emotional withdrawal used as a weapon to hurt someone. Punishment answers the question 'How do I make you feel what I feel?' It shows up as silent treatment, saying 'I'm done' to create fear of loss, and withholding affection to teach a lesson."

"Lets see, here's an example: Hanging up and blocking someone mid-argument to make them panic or feel dismissed. Or exclaiming "Fine. I just won't tell you anything anymore' to make the other person feel bad for having an opinion or starting a difficult conversation. How have you used a boundary as a punishment?"

Someone said, "I used silence as protection, but it became punishment."

Another woman said through tears. "I didn't realize until now that I use anger as a boundary because I never learned a healthy one. I would hold on to all the pain and then blow up on the person, cut them out of my life, and call my anger protecting my peace."

There was agreement, hugs, and women softly expressing their knowingness.

Finally, Simone said, "I get loud, have a short temper, or become petty. It's mainly because I don't know how to say, 'I'm scared you're going to leave me' or 'I need more from you'. So, I protect myself before anyone gets a chance to hurt me."

Traci lightly rubbed her shoulder. "Simone, boundaries do not end relationships. They should reveal which ones can survive honesty." Traci walked the circle of chairs slowly.

"These are not personality flaws," she said. "These are survival strategies. Tonight, we're not judging them. We're just done letting them run wild, unchallenged." She had everyone fold their paper. "Pair up," she said. "If you're brave enough, share one boundary you've violated against yourself."

The room filled with shuffling chairs and quiet murmurs. A younger woman named Bri slid near Keischa. "Can we partner?" she asked.

"Yeah," Keischa replied and read her own whisper-written line aloud, "I allowed inconsistency because I feared rejection more than I feared losing myself."

Bri winced in solidarity. "Girl, that's deep. I wrote, I let silence be my excuse," she said. "Like if I don't say nothing, I can't mess up."

Across the room, Simone's voice was shaking as she told an older woman, "I let people pour and pour into me, but only if it means they still need me. If I'm not needed, I don't know who I am."

The older woman nodded like she'd been there, done that, burned the T-shirt. "That's not love, baby. That's emotional employment. Too much invisible labor."

Traci ended the workshop with a statement that felt like transformation for Keischa, "Remember, ladies," she said as she leaned in. "A boundary isn't a punishment. It's a standard. A self-honoring. And it will expose who can love you in a healthy way."

"I heard there was once someone who asked, 'How long can I keep giving and giving and disrespecting my boundaries?' The answer was poetic, 'How long can you keep drinking poison before you die?'"

A tear slid down Keischa's cheek. "Can I ask you something?" she whispered. "Why do boundaries feel like I'm doing something wrong?"

Traci didn't hesitate. "Because as a Black woman, you were raised in systems that benefited from you having none." Silence. Gut-punching silence.

"But you're rewriting that," Traci said. "Every time you choose yourself. Your boundaries are you saying 'I am choosing me.'"

The sun was low by the time Keischa stepped outside the community center. Not quite sunset, but that soft hour before it. When the world starts winding down, but isn't quite ready to rest. The wind was gentle, warm, almost congratulatory.

She walked slowly to her car, each step feeling different than the one before it. What was this? She felt lighter, grounded, like her body, thoughts, and soul finally belonged to her.

Malcolm

Malcolm sat in his car at a stoplight on the way to his apartment the same night of the latest workshop. He was scrolling through social media, pretending not to notice he hadn't heard from Keischa since early morning.

He didn't like it. Not because he missed her, though he did, but because her silence unnerved him. She was supposed to be reachable. Predictable. Available. His soft landing. His peace. Instead, she felt the opposite of what he needed. Unavailable. Missing. His chest tightened in a way he didn't recognize. Fear mixed with the discomfort of her pulling away, going silent, and stepping out of the pattern he depended on her for.

A memory flickered. He was seven watching his mother cry at the kitchen sink while his father walked out with barely a word. No boundaries. No expectations. No stability. Even at seven years old, he had learned that love was not stable and could just up and leave. The lesson was it is always better to leave before you could be left. Malcolm sighed and was brought back from his thoughts when a car horn blew, altering him that the light had turned green. He ran a hand over his face.

"Damn," he muttered. "She been going to these workshops and therapy. It feels like she leaving me behind. She changing." The thing he feared most wasn't losing her. It was her learning she didn't have to chase him. He picked up his phone and texted her once again.

Keischa had learned to put her phone up when she walked in the house to spend time with the kids, start her routine, and take time with herself. Read, listen to music, eat a meal at the table, or just chill. The minute she picked up the phone, the notifications came through: (2) messages. Rayna, dang. Keischa had forgotten about her. And Malcolm. She read Rayna's text first.

"Hey, girl. I need a favor. I'm about to get evicted and I know you always have my back. I need a couple of dollars and a place to crash while I'm here. Hit me back."

That was it. No "How are you?" No connection. Just the usual need and want. Her childhood ghost. Her inherited wound. Her first emotional debt collector.

Keischa began typing readily, but shakily, "I love you. I really, really do. And you did the best you could with what you had, but I can't be your survival plan anymore. I'm not leaving you," Keischa continued typing, "but I'm not losing myself for you either."

As Keischa typed something was breaking open and something else was finally loosening. "And if you want to stay in my life," Keischa continued typing, hands steady as breath, "it can't be on the terms of fourteen-year-old me. I'm grown now. I get to choose how I'm loved. I'm choosing how I allow people to treat me and how I treat myself. I've learned that boundaries don't remove people. They remove dysfunction. I don't have the space or energy to be your help. I deserve better than that. Love you and hope everything works out. Best Keisch."

Her thoughts raced, her energy shifted, and her stomach did a flip, but through it all she still hit send. Phew! Now, for Malcolm. He had texted one line after being unavailable again. Even after all the conversations and promises. Keischa was mad and disappointed. Not so much at him, but at herself.

The truth is she knew better. This ghosting, disappearing, popping in and out was as much her fault as his. The first time he was out of contact for a couple of hours, then one day, then a week, and then weeks completely ghost became his routine.

She had let this be the pattern, the routine, the normal, and the green light to keep doing it. Now, here they were again. His silence and manipulation, and her feeling disposable. She no longer was willing to do the no-call no-show for two weeks and then pop up as if nothing ever happened, again.

Still, when she saw his text, "Can we talk?" the old familiar pull surged through her body and softened her, but her new tools taught her this pattern of their relationship no longer fit who she was. She typed slowly, holding her breath, "I'm not available to talk right now. I need space."

She stared at it. Her heart raced. Traci's words echoed in her head, the boundary quiz that she took surfaced. She reviewed the text, closed her eyes, took a deep breath and then hit send. And for the first time in her life, she realized that her world didn't end. Her body didn't crumble. Her spirit didn't shrink. She felt lighter. Stronger. Present. She whispered quietly, "Look at me choosing me."

The Therapy Session

Two days later, in Traci's office, the eucalyptus smell felt grounding. Everything felt comfortable and safe. As Keischa settled into her favorite big comfortable chair, she steadied herself for her session.

"So," Traci asked, "did you respond to Malcolm?"

"Dang, girl! No small talk? No 'what up doe?'" Keischa said laughing, "We getting straight to it, huh? So, yeah. I answered his text after the boundary workshop. For once, when I texted him back I didn't feel like my world would be shaken. I didn't feel like I would be taking a L. It felt like I had a choice in my life."

"How did that feel?"

Terrifying. Liberating. Lonely. Empowering. All at once. Keischa stared out the window.

"Part of me wanted to run back to the pattern," she said. "The other part, the part of me that's growing and moving up the pyramid, and that's falling in love with myself said, 'Um...yeah, boy. Not this time.'"

Traci smiled gently. "That part is your boundary voice. It's the adult you, protecting the child you." Keischa nodded, feeling tears sting the back of her eyes.

"It's wild how this work has changed me. Oh, wait! I didn't tell you! A family member from the past came back into my life. I was able to set a boundary and move forward without wanting her in my life. And I made a note," Keischa paused to pull out her phone and check what she wrote. "I wanted to ask you to expound on what you meant when we talked about how, 'Unhealed relationships don't disappear. They calcify into belief systems.'"

"Okay, yes! Let's get into it," Traci laughed. "Look at you."

"I know, right?!" Keisha began giggling. "I'm definitely feeling this new version of me, but I need expansion on this. What did you mean?"

"Ok, sooo let's talk it out. When unhealed relationships harden into our belief systems, it means past traumas shape our core views of ourselves and others. These patterns become deeply ingrained patterns that can affect trust, self-worth, and how we connect with others. It's crazy because this can happen without us even realizing it. When we don't examine or identify these issues, we become rigid, fixed, and inflexible. When relationship wounds are unhealed, they can affect how we set boundaries and how we protect ourselves."

Keischa wanted to dance around that office, all she needed was some confetti and a glass of champagne. She said to Tracie, "Baybee this is good. I was able to step out of what was, and decide what I want in my life. I'm literally starting to change narratives, make boundaries, and understand who I am. Ok, let's move forward and talk about this self-actualization."

For the first time, Keischa felt like she was not on the hamster wheel. Walking to the parking lot after her session she thought, *"Why don't they teach this in school? I am so grateful for my becoming!"* She climbed into her car, looked in the review mirror to smile at herself, and liked the reflection she saw.

Tools

1. Boundary Mapping Exercise

Which of these categories of boundaries protects my peace? Which protects my patterns?

    1.Non-negotiable boundaries

2. Flexible boundaries

3. Growing-edge boundaries

2. The "Body First" Boundary Check

Before saying "yes" or "no" to a request, pause and ask your body: "Where do I feel this?"

- Tight chest = obligation
- Stomach flip = anxiety
- Open breath = alignment
  Choose accordingly.

3. The Attachment-Safe Sentence Starter

Use this when setting boundaries with people you care about:
"I'm choosing this boundary to honor myself, not to distance myself from you."

4. Maslow's Ladder Daily Check-In

Does this request or relationship support my:

- Safety?
- Belonging?
- Esteem?

If it doesn't support the bottom three tiers of Maslow's pyramid, your "yes" is probably a bargain with self-abandonment.

Affirmations for Boundaries

- I am worthy of relationships that honor my needs.
- Saying "no" is a full sentence and a full act of self-love.
- My boundaries protect what I am growing into.
- I do not have to earn my rest, safety, or dignity.
- I can love others without betraying myself.

Scripture for Reflection

"Above all else, guard your heart, for everything you do flows from it." Proverbs 4:23

Chapter Eleven

Self-Love and Forgiveness

"Forgiveness is not about what they deserve. It's about what you no longer want to carry." — Shaaree McCalpine

Keischa

Keischa didn't realize how addicted she had been to people pleasing and validating others. It had been veiled as "being there for others", "that's just who I am", or "I'm a good person." That is, until she started healing.

It wasn't loud at first. It was in small moments that would've seemed normal to anyone else. Looking in the mirror she seemed confident, but what wasn't seen was how she automatically looked for what needed fixing. Like the way she replayed conversations in her head, not to understand them, but to find the moment she "messed up." Like the way she made a mistake at work and immediately felt shame rise up. She would feel the need to apologize or fix the problem, even if it wasn't her fault. She felt the shame of needing to be perfect, to do better. She took on ownership and felt the need to make "it better". It's crazy how when you start to understand things and learn new emotional tools you realize what's not yours to own.

She was standing in her kitchen when it hit her. The late morning light was pouring in, soft and golden, hitting the countertop like a quiet blessing. She liked the crackling sound of the wooden wick candle and she loved the new discoveries of the little things that brought her joy. It made the house feel alive and comfortable. Her scents were always something earthy, cedar, and tobacco. She chuckled because she was never a sweet scent girlie. Strawberry poundcake, vanilla, and cookie crumble were never her thing. Laughing out loud, she thought Traci would say she was in her "grounded era". She wasn't quite sure of that because she had always loved those scents. Coffee houses were her favorite.

Her phone was on the counter, face down. She had done that on purpose. Her therapy had taught her this, she learned it created space and boundaries. Before, the phone was like a leash. It kept her available, useful, and needed. Now, she was learning the difference between connection and obligation. It still felt strange. Like wearing a new pair of shoes that were cute, but stiff. You had to break them boys in before they stopped rubbing your heels raw. LOL! Thinking about this cracked her up. She remembered going to a concert, leaving out not being able to find her car, and literally having her feet bleed walking through the parking structure. Cute, but not never again.

She poured coffee into her mug, took one sip, then another. No rush. No mental checklist. She thought about Maslow and the way Traci drew that pyramid with confidence like she had known it her whole life. Keischa used to live at the bottom of it. Survival. Safety. Trying to make love feel secure by working hard enough for it. Now she was hovering higher up, sometimes steady, sometimes shaky. It was a balance between esteem and self-actualization. She definitely did not feel desperation. Her happier life was feeling like reality. She was learning how to live. How to give herself the energy she gave others. She started to wipe down the counters for no reason other than her hands had gotten used to routine and rhythm. She caught herself and stopped intentionally. Simone texted her right on cue.

Simone, "You home? I'm outside. Open the door." Keischa laughed, loud enough that it startled her a little. Keischa loved how comfortable the relationship was. Simone usually stopped by on Saturdays as she called it Sister Saturdays. It felt good to be valued, understood, and just loved. When she opened the door, Simone stood there with two bags– one from a Black-owned breakfast spot and one from a grocery store. She had on an oversized hoodie, hoops, and that look in her eyes that meant she was trying to be brave without letting anyone know.

"You brought groceries?" Keischa asked. Simone rolled her eyes. "Girl, yes. Because I'm trying to be a better person and not just show up with hot food and trauma." Keischa stepped aside, letting her in. Simone paused for a second like she was taking in the peace of the space: the soft throw blanket, the neat counters, the way Keischa's home always smelled like she had just finished praying and baking.

"You got your candle going again," Simone said.

Keischa shrugged. "It calms me."

Simone nodded, "Girl, that's cool, but the aesthetic sometimes makes me wanna mess something up. You know, so it's not so umm... perfect."

Keischa blinked, then laughed, "Girl you bet'not. And don't act like you don't love it."

They sat, laughed, and ate at the kitchen table. Simone tried to keep it light, but her fingers kept tapping the table like she was waiting for the perfect opening to say what she was really thinking.

Keischa didn't rush her, which was new for her. She usually hated waiting for information. Finally, Simone exhaled like she was jumping off a cliff.

"I've been thinking about forgiveness," she said.

Keischa lifted her eyebrows, "Okay."

Simone stared down at her plate. "I'm realizing I don't forgive myself for who I had to become."

Keischa's chest tightened.

Simone's voice got quieter. "I've been carrying this feeling like I've always done too much. Like I should've been softer, sweeter, more trusting. But I couldn't. I had a mama who checked out emotionally right when I needed her. A father who left. A house where being sensitive got you ignored." Keischa watched her friend's face as she spoke, noticing how Simone's eyes got glassy, but her jaw stayed clenched like she was still trying to hold it all in.

Simone kept going, and her voice started to shake. "I remember being ten. I had won an award at school. I came home so excited. I ran into the kitchen like, 'Ma, look!' And she didn't even turn around. She was stirring a pot, saying, 'That's great. That's what you always do.'

Simone swallowed hard. "I stood there holding that paper until my hands got sweaty. Then I walked to my room and taped it to the wall myself." Keischa felt tears sting her eyes. Simone shook her head. At this big grown age, she was disgusted with how much she still cared.

She continued, "So I stopped expecting. I became sarcastic. Hard. The strong friend. The funny friend. The one who could take a joke. The one who didn't need anything." She finally looked up at Keischa. "But I did need love. And I hated myself for it."

Keischa reached across the table and held her hand. "Simone," she whispered. "You don't have to hate her anymore. That little girl."

Simone's eyes filled and spilled. "I don't know how to stop."

Keischa squeezed her hand. "We practice. We go to therapy. I know you think therapy isn't necessary, I thought that too, but it saved my life."

Simone laughed through tears, "You sound like Traci."

Keischa smiled softly, then surprised herself by saying, "I sound like healing."

Keischa

The following week Keischa did a little smile as she pulled on some comfy clothes and gazed around her quiet room. She was so thankful she had taken today off– no explanation, no guilt, no apologies. This was just for her. She reviewed her to-do list and the schedule for Traci's workshops. When she saw the topic for the next one she paused. "Wait... what does this say? Forgiveness! Mann, God really be eavesdropping," Keischa said out loud to no one. "I can't wait for this."

"Forgiveness, hmmm." It took her back to her last text to Rayna. It's crazy she hadn't even responded. At her next therapy session, Keischa would talk to Traci about how she still felt nervous and anxious, waiting for Rayna to respond. For most of her life, silence felt dangerous, hurtful. If someone went quiet, ghosted her, gave her the silent treatment, or didn't answer fast enough she assumed she had done something wrong and would instantly go into repair mode.

But right now, Keischa was feeling ah-ma-zing! She grabbed her phone to post an inspirational video, when she got a message that felt like a slap in the face. Hard. Rayna had responded. The text wasn't a conversation. No apologies, no tears, no moment of understanding, or asking questions. It was sharp, unfiltered, and painful.

Keischa blinked, swallowed hard and held back tears as she read, "You are so selfish. I shouldn't be surprised, that's who you are. Everything is always about you. And this supposed healing?! You have never thought about how what you do affects anybody else. You disgust me. And now I remember why I don't fuck with you. Still a loser. Don't call or text me. You are blocked. I HATE YOU!!!"

Keischa read it once. Then again. Her chest tightened with that familiar reflex activating before she could stop it — the urge to defend, to explain, to make herself small enough to be palatable again. She could already hear the words forming in her head, *"That's not what I meant. I wasn't trying to hurt you."*

She sat down on the edge of the bed instead of texting back. The room felt quiet in a way that pressed against her ribs. Not peaceful. Not yet. Just still enough for the truth to surface. Rayna hadn't blocked her because Keischa was cruel. Rayna had blocked her because Keischa was unavailable for the role she used to play. That realization hurt more than the text itself.

Keischa placed one hand on her chest, the other on her stomach, and breathed slowly grounding herself the way Traci had taught her. She named what was there instead of fighting it– hurt, grief, and disappointment.

She didn't rush to soothe it. She didn't override it with logic, or scripture, or gratitude. She let it exist without turning it into proof that she was wrong. She opened her journal and wrote one sentence, "I can be loving without being available for harm." She shed tears, prayed, gathered her breathing and closed the journal and that chapter of her life. And for the first time in her life, she didn't respond to Rayna.

That night, after the house settled into sleep, Keischa stood in the doorway of her daughter's room. Haven was curled on her side, one arm flung over her pillow, breathing slow and even. LOL, it tickled Keischa to watch her sleep. She had always slept wild, utilizing the whole bed. Across the hall, her son Devin murmured softly in his sleep.

"Mom?" Haven whispered suddenly, eyes fluttering open.

Keischa stepped inside. "Hey, baby, what's wrong?"

"You're happier lately," Haven said, voice thick with sleep. "You don't yell as much. You aren't mean." The words landed harder than any therapy insight ever had.

Keischa swallowed. "How does that feel?"

Haven shrugged. "Calmer, happier, nicer. Maybe... I think... I feel loved."

Keischa kissed her forehead and said, "That's because I do love you," and turned off the light, her throat tight.

This was the cost-benefit analysis no worksheet could capture. She wasn't just healing for herself anymore. That was crazy because she hadn't thought about it like that. It was crazy that her actions had affected the kids. The very people she was trying to build a good life for.

That revelation was still sitting in her spirit, as she closed Haven's door and walked toward the kitchen. When notifications lit up her phone, she was fearful to even look at it. Praying it wouldn't be Rayna. She really wasn't up for another one of those messages. That light flashing reminded her to delete that contact. She pulled the phone out of her robe pocket. Not Rayna, but still a disruption to her nervous system: Malcolm.

"Miss you."

Just two words. Simple. Heavy. Keischa stared at the screen. The old pattern, longing, and the pull on her heart came up. The pull that signaled that he was in control of her emotions and desires. Her body reacted. Her breathing quickened and her shoulders felt heavy with the urgency of having him back in her life.

She thought about the way Malcolm held her waist when he walked past her in the kitchen like he couldn't help himself. The way he called her "Keisch" like it was a prayer. The way he looked at her like she was the best thing since the frosted honey bun. Times when love wasn't all bad. The moments when his softness and laughter made her feel safe and content.

Then she thought about the other things. How he disappeared when she needed him most. How he apologized and repeated the same thing over and over. How his love sometimes felt like a door that only opened when he felt like walking through it. The inconsistency that always left her feeling worthless and made her think she needed to be better. That she needed to prove she was worthy of his interest and love.

Keischa placed the phone down on the kitchen countertop, looked at the ceiling, and whispered, "God, help me. I don't want to be stupid." Then she corrected herself out loud. "I don't want to shame myself." She was learning forgiveness and growth was also about the language you used with yourself. She closed her eyes, took a deep breath and then dialed his number.

"I miss you," Malcolm said immediately. "I know I messed up, but I'm trying."

She leaned against the counter, eyes closed. The old Keischa would've melted.

"I know you're trying," she said. "But effort without consistency still hurts."

Silence.

"You're really done?" he asked.

Tears burned her eyes. She had that familiar lump in her throat. The kind that you grapple with to speak, but you still can't.

"Yes," she said but it did come out strong. It wasn't convincing. She didn't even believe it, but she continued, "I don't want to keep begging you to love me, to consider me, to value me. I won't beg anyone anymore. I deserve better. I chose more."

"I know, love. That's why I'm calling. Let me show you better."

"No," she said steadily. "I'm not going to abandon myself to stay connected to you. And I forgive myself for doing that in the past, but I won't repeat it." Her voice cracked, but she didn't retreat. "I'm not available for half-love anymore."

"Okay, Keisch, I'll move around. Like I said, I just wanted you to know I wanted to try again. I miss you and I love you." Click.

Keischa slid down the kitchen wall and cried. Not because she doubted the choice, but because growth still grieves. With all the healing and revelation, it still hurt. It hurt bad. She looked at the phone, reread his message, "I miss you", then threw the phone across the room. *Damn, why can't you just love me?"* she questioned.

Keischa woke up the next morning, late, a mess, and unable to focus. She even yelled at the kids, something she hadn't done in months. She called off work and dropped the kids off at school. She got right back in the bed, stared at the phone, cried, screamed, and cried some more.

"I hate this", she said loudly. "He loves me, he just don't know how to show it. Maybe if I..." her thoughts were interrupted by a calendar reminder for her therapy session. She turned off the sound and went to sleep, exhausted.

Simone

A week later, Simone sat in her apartment staring out of the window holding a cold cup of coffee. She was trying to sort out her feelings. Ever since she and Keischa had become close, she had looked forward to their Saturday kick-it. The comfort of the apartment, the food, the ability to open up. It had not been easy growing close to her, but at almost a year in it felt natural. They felt like sisters.

Yet, this Saturday felt heavy. There was no get-together. She had texted Keischa last Friday and this Friday. Still, she hadn't gotten a text back. She had called and it went to voicemail. What had she done? Was Keischa mad at her? Was she too clingy? Did Keisch want distance? The thoughts ran rampant in her head. She was snapped back to reality by the disgusting cold coffee in her cup touching her tongue. Simone longed for good coffee and good conversation. Which brought her back to Keischa. She would normally be at her house rehashing the week, eating, and drinking hot coffee. She didn't know if she should feel hurt, angry, or abandoned. She lit the candle Keisch had purchased for her and cuddled up on the couch feeling alone.

"I wonder where Traci would say I was on the pyramid?" She laughed at how far she had come by attending the workshops. Simone tried to reassure herself that she could handle this shift even as she felt her soul shake. "It's cool, Keisch wants space. Bet, she got it."

Keischa

It was Saturday, again. Two weeks had gone by without a peep from Malcolm. It was getting easier for her to tolerate his absence. The only thing was she still felt anticipation of him popping up at the house, a call, or text. And just like that, like the phone could read her thoughts,

"Hey." A text from Malcolm.

"Hey," she texted back way too fast. *"Damn, girl, why did you do that? Now it looks like you've been sitting by the phone waiting. Ugh,"* she thought.

Malcom: "You think you could make time for me today? I've been going crazy without you Keisch."

She could see his smile through the phone. She really wanted to stay strong. To tell him "GTFOH". She typed slowly, "Nah, I'm good. I'm not here for the rollercoaster ride with you. The inconsistency. I know my worth." She smiled at the message, read it out loud. "Dang, Keischa, you a Boss," she said proudly. Then erased it and typed, "Yes, I miss you too." Send.

Malcolm showed up that night with food in hand, flowers, and that beautiful, captivating smile. He looked good. Too good. He was shaved, smelled good, and dressed like he had somewhere important to be.

Keischa slid into the chair across from him and immediately noticed how her heart skipped a beat. The way his fingers tapped the table. The way he smiled slowly at her, felt like his embrace.

He reached for her hand. She let him hold it just for a second. She hated how good it felt. *"Stay strong, Keischa,"* she internally instructed herself. *"Let's take this slow."*

Malcolm sighed. "I've been doing a lot of thinking."

Keischa nodded. "That makes two of us," she said lightly, but her eyes stayed serious.

He smiled, then his face fell. "No, for real. I want to try again. Intentionally. I'm tired of ruining good things because I don't know how to stay."

Keischa's heart fluttered. This is what she had been wanting to hear. Is this for real? "What does trying look like?" she asked.

Malcolm paused. That pause was familiar. He exhaled. "I don't have all the words. I just know I don't want to lose you. We can take time to figure that out together. You been going to therapy. Maybe that."

Keischa leaned back slightly. Not fully believing his words or promises, but desperately wanting to. Malcolm sat up as if he could read her mind. "I'm choosing you, love, I'm choosing us."

Keischa studied him. "Okay," she said slowly. "Then consistency, not sporadic attendance, plus real consideration and understanding is what I need."

Malcolm swallowed hard. And in that swallow Keischa saw it, fear. The attachment wound and the part of him that wanted love, but didn't trust it.

Malcolm

Malcolm stared out the window for a second and it felt like his mind had gone somewhere else. He was twelve, standing on the porch steps with a duffel bag in his hand because his father said they were going fishing. His mother had braided his hair extra neat that morning like she didn't want his father to see how desperate she was for him to show up. His father pulled up two hours late, music blasting, laughing like he hadn't just made a child wait with hope sweating in his hands.

"Come on, lil man," his father said. "Stop acting like a girl."

Malcolm got in the car and smiled like it didn't hurt. They didn't go fishing. His father dropped him off at his auntie's house and disappeared for three days. When he came back, he bought Malcolm a new pair of shoes and acted like the shoes erased the abandonment.

His mother whispered later, "Just forgive him, Malcolm. He's trying." Malcolm learned forgiveness as a form of self-abandonment. He learned that love came with disappearing acts. He learned to be ready for disappointment, so it wouldn't break him. Malcolm's eyes were glossy when he turned his focus back to Keischa.

"I don't know if I've forgiven my dad for not being consistent," he admitted. "Or if I just stopped expecting anything from him or anybody."

Keischa felt the urge to rescue him, to hold him, to fix it rise in her chest. She didn't. That was self-love too.

"I'm sorry," she said softly. "I really am."

Malcolm nodded. "And I'm sorry for doing that to you."

They sat in that truth. Then he leaned forward. "I want to do better, Keisch. I do."

Keischa's voice was gentle, but firm, "Then we try again. But slow. And if the red flags show up again, I'm not going to hate myself for leaving."

Malcolm looked down. "Fair."

Keischa sighed and smiled softly, "And I'm not going to hate myself for trying either." That landed differently for her. That was forgiveness, in real time, for herself. Not him.

Workshop Day

The workshop that following week was packed and the energy felt different. Growth had changed the room's posture. Besides the energy and anticipation, Keischa also noticed something was different with Simone. She had tried calling her back with no response. It was strange she hadn't heard from her all week, but maybe she needed space or just wanted time to herself. She could definitely relate.

Dealing with the job, the kids, and Malcolm had really landed heavily. Now at the workshop, Simone seemed angry, distant. She had given a half-wave when she entered and sat on the other side of the room. Seeing her sitting on the edge of the chair felt odd. Keischa decided that she would check in with her after the workshop, this wasn't the time or place.

Traci walked in wearing a soft black jumpsuit, hair pulled back, gold hoops, eyes steady. She looked like a woman who had survived and still had softness left. She didn't play with her intro. She went straight for the heart.

"Today we're talking about self-love, forgiveness and their part in thriving," she said. "And before anybody starts thinking forgiveness is about being nice," she laughed that beautiful silky laugh, "let me correct that. Let's talk about where self-love actually lives. Not in affirmations. Not taking long bubble baths. But the kind of self-understanding that changes behavior."

A few women chuckled knowingly. The whiteboard behind her held the familiar shape, our beloved pyramid, but this time, it wasn't drawn neatly. The lines were uneven, layered, and almost messy. Traci began, "You don't climb this once. You move through it again and again. Thriving is knowing how to come back to yourself when you slip. We've talked about safety. Love. Worth. Anger. Attachment. Rest. Boundaries. And today, self-love and forgiveness." She paused, scanning the room.

She tapped the middle of the pyramid. "But this stage, Belonging and Esteem, is where a lot of us get stuck. Especially, Black women." Heads nodded.

"Because we confuse being needed with being loved," Traci continued. "We confuse endurance with commitment. And attachment wounds make us believe that choosing ourselves means abandoning others."

She handed out some half slips of paper. "Quick exercise," she said. "Circle the statements that feel familiar."

Keischa scanned the page:
- I feel guilty when I don't respond right away.
- I explain my boundaries more than necessary.
- I confuse discomfort with danger.
- I stay longer than I should to avoid being seen as 'too much.'

Her pen hovered, then circled more than she expected. Across the room, Simone exhaled sharply, shaking her head, "Damn."

Traci smiled gently. "Awareness isn't indictment. It's an invitation to embrace it." She turned back to the board. "The self-actualization level isn't where you stop wanting love. It's where you stop sacrificing yourself to earn it."

The room grew quiet with anticipation, everyone seemed eager to hear what was next and how it could help empower their lives.

"Attachment patterns as we talked about previously, for those who are new see me later so you can take the attachment quiz, show up here because this is the stage where old patterns either loosen their grip or tighten it."

Keischa felt the words settle in her body, not as theory, but as lived truth. They hit hard, because now she was thinking about how she had let

Malcolm back in her life. Was it a betrayal of her self-love? She scribbled it in her notebook to bring up in therapy.

Traci continued, "Self-actualization is the level where you stop living your life based on old wounds. But hear me clearly, self-actualization doesn't mean you never dip back down. It means you have a home base now. You know where you belong."

She moved her finger down to Esteem and Belonging. "Forgiveness often lives right here," she said, tapping the middle. "Because we forgive to preserve connection. We forgive, so we don't get abandoned. We forgive because being liked feels like safety."

Simone's throat tightened.

Traci continued, "But self-love and forgiveness is different. It's not about 'them'. It's about you not betraying yourself anymore."

A woman across the circle raised her hand, "Don't kill me, Traci, but here's the question. What if I don't believe self-love is real?"

The room felt a collective moment of breath-holding. As they waited for the response.

Traci nodded. "Say more."

The woman swallowed. "I've seen sacrifice. I've seen survival. I've seen women stay tired and call it strength. But I've never actually seen self-love lived out."

A murmur rippled through the room.

Simone felt like this was her moment. She felt seen, understood, and connected and before she could talk herself out of it, she raised her hand.

"I don't know if it exists either," Simone said, her voice already shaking. "Not in real life. Not for women like me."

All eyes turned toward her.

"My mom never chose herself," Simone continued. "She stayed. She endured. She died tired. And people called her strong. It felt like they loved her because of this strength."

Her voice cracked. "So, when y'all talk about self-love, part of me wants to believe it. But another part of me thinks it's just another thing we're supposed to figure out alone."

Tears spilled freely now, from Simone and other women in the workshop.

"I don't even know what it looks like to love myself without feeling selfish or unsafe. I've never seen it modeled. Ever," Simone concluded.

The room held space for her. Nodding, agreeing, and understanding.

Traci stepped closer, her voice gentle but grounded. "That makes sense," she said. "You can't trust what you've never witnessed." She turned to the group.

"For many of us, self-love feels false or like betrayal. We were taught that love means staying even when it costs us ourselves. We've seen this through real life examples, quotes, and sayings that were passed down through generations. Even now, anyone with a social platform makes it hard to move in a way that benefits self without guilt. Traci paused, her eyes shifting like she was deciding whether to share something personal. The room held its breath. "I'm going to tell y'all something I've never said out loud," she said quietly.

Traci swallowed. "I used to punish myself for needing love. Self-love is forgiving yourself for being human."

That line cracked the room open. Simone's tears fell quietly. Keischa felt her own chest expand like she could breathe again.

She stared at the floor for a second, then looked up. The room leaned in.

"I stayed in a relationship that was wrong for me for years," Traci said quietly. "Not because I didn't know better, but because I didn't know how to forgive the part of me that wanted love so badly, I was willing to disappear and shrink."

A few women gasped softly.

"Ladies, let's pair up for this exercise. It's designed to identify the places you shrink for connection in relationships. It is called 'I Shrink When

______.'" They were instructed to fill in the blank honestly, and out loud with their partner.

Keischa and Simone paired up.

"I hate this," Simone whispered with a nervous smile.

"Same," Keischa replied. "It's like I'm naked when we share our emotions out loud."

After a few minutes in the pairs, Traci began, "Does anyone feel safe enough to share?"

Simone went first. "I shrink when I feel replaceable."

"And you Keischa, would you want to share? No pressure."

Keischa swallowed. "I shrink when I feel like love is conditional."

The room felt still. Simone blurted out. "I thought healing meant I wouldn't get triggered anymore. I don't think I'm thriving. I still feel like it's easy for people to abandon me. If I stop being useful, people will stop choosing me and ignore me. I know that's my stuff. I just haven't unlearned it yet."

Simone's voice trembled. "Sometimes, Keisch you can shut down. Like when you suddenly cancelled our get-together two Saturdays in a row. When you pull back, I feel like I'm bothering you."

Keischa inhaled sharply. Her chest tightened.

Traci interjected calmly, "And this is a moment where we see relational rupture. But thriving isn't about mastering these things. It's about moving through them without losing yourself."

Keischa felt that land in her chest.

Traci continued, "Self-actualization doesn't mean you live at the top of Maslow's pyramid. It means you know how to come back to yourself no matter where you land. Go ahead and share what you feel, Simone. We are here to listen."

Murmurs of agreement surrounded her. "Say that, girl!" a woman called out, which encouraged Simone to continue.

"The last two weeks," Simone continued without censoring herself, "Keischa didn't hang out with me, or text me back and I spiraled. I thought you were pulling away."

There it was. The reason why Simone had been so distant today. Keischa's stomach dropped.

Traci spoke into the tension, "This is part of the process of discovering self and attachment wounds. Thriving requires growth, but it happens at our own pace. Now, Keischa. Tell Simone what you want to say. Not perfectly, just honestly."

Simone turned to Keischa. The room was still.

"I was going through some tough things that day. I was overwhelmed and didn't want to talk, or do anything based on obligation. I'm not doing that anymore. So, I took space. But I know I have a tendency to shut down and pull back when I'm scared," Keischa said. "Not because I don't care. I shrink back for my protection. I also understand that I still could have communicated that I needed space. I know how ghosting feels. I don't want to ever feel disposable, so I don't want to make anyone else, especially a friend, feel like that. I thought our friendship was strong enough for you to understand that, but I understand that wasn't for you to carry. I'm sorry."

Silence. Then Simone nodded slowly, her eyes filled with tears. "I don't want us to repeat what hurt us. That scared me, but I'm working on it for real, for real. I still panic when closeness shifts." Simone felt herself laugh-talking through the tears. "Dang, Traci, I just flashed back to the workshop that taught me my attachment style responds to distance as danger. Phew, I'm sorry Keischa for putting that on you."

Keischa reached for her hand, "I know. I'm here now."

That exchange, raw, imperfect, and vulnerable, landed harder than any lecture.

Traci watched quietly, then said to the room, "Y'all see this? This is secure attachment in action. That is relational repair. This is what relational healing looks like. It's not perfect. It's honesty that risks loss. Not avoiding rupture, but repairing it."

Then she turned the workshop inward. "I want you all to think about one place in your life where you're still surviving or struggling while we work on the next exercise," Traci said as she handed out a sheet titled 'The Forgiveness Map: Where are you stuck?'

Simone exhaled joking, "Shoot! I'm going to sit this one out. I'm spent." The room burst out in laughter and turned back to their partner. Keischa laughed along.

Traci smiled softly and said, "That's growth."

"Write down the version of yourself you hate," Traci instructed gently. "The one you call stupid. The one you call weak. The one you judge."

Keischa's pen hovered. She wrote: The version of me that stayed too long.

Simone wrote: The version of me that needed people.

Traci's voice softened, "Now, write what she was trying to protect."

Keischa's hand shook as she wrote: She was trying to be chosen.

Simone wrote: She was trying not to be abandoned.

Traci nodded like she expected the responses she saw on the papers around her. "That's attachment," she says. "That's the nervous system choosing survival strategies. Forgiveness is you saying to that part of yourself, 'Thank you for protecting me. I got it now.'"

Keischa felt chills. Simone put her hand over her chest.

"Y'all," Simone whispered, voice cracking, "I've been mad at myself for wanting love."

Traci stepped closer. "And what if wanting love is not your weakness? What if it's your humanity?"

Simone broke down. Keischa pulled her in, holding her like a sister holds a sister. No fixing, no shame. Just presence. And in that moment, Keischa knew this was the feeling of thriving. Not the absence of pain, but the presence of safe love.

The Therapy Session

A few days later, Keischa sat on Traci's couch, legs tucked under her like she belonged there. The eucalyptus smell was familiar. Comforting. She let her shoulders relax.

Traci smiled. "So, how's the Malcolm situation?"

Keischa laughed nervously, "Girl, we trying."

Traci nodded. "And how you treating yourself in the middle of it?"

Keischa hesitated. "Better. I'm not calling myself stupid."

Traci leaned in. "Good. Because self-actualization is not you becoming perfect. It's you becoming honest without abandoning yourself."

Keischa swallowed. "Sometimes, I still feel shaky and scared."

Traci nodded. "Of course you do. Attachment doesn't disappear. It gets reassured. It gets rewired."

Keischa looked down at her hands. "So, in this situation forgiveness is...?"

Traci's voice was soft. "Forgiveness is you refusing to punish yourself for what you didn't know then. And refusing to repeat those mistakes, knowing what you know now."

Keischa felt tears rise. "So, is it ok that I want to try again?" she whispered. "And I can still be healed?"

"Yes," Traci said. "As long as you choose yourself while you try."

That hit like truth. Keischa exhaled, "I'm learning how to love me while I love somebody else."

Traci smiled. "That's the top of the pyramid, baby."

Keischa laughed through tears. "Don't call me baby. I'll cry more."

Traci chuckled. "Cry. That's self-love too."

At home that night, Keischa sat at her desk and wrote a letter to herself. Not a long one. Just real.

Dear Keischa,

I forgive you for hoping.

I forgive you for trying.

I forgive you for being human.

You are not stupid. You are learning.

And you are safe with me now.

She folded it, placed it in her journal, and whispered quietly, "I'm not at the bottom anymore." And, the hot tea was, she believed herself.

Supportive Tools for the Reader: Self-love + Forgiveness

1. The Self-Forgiveness Script (Say It Out Loud)

When you catch yourself calling yourself "stupid," "weak," or "too much," replace it with:

- "I did the best I could with what I knew."
- "I'm not stupid. I'm learning."
- "I can choose better now without shaming who I was then."

2. The Forgiveness Map Exercise

Write the version of yourself that you often judge. Then answer:

- What was she trying to protect?
- What did she believe she had to do to be loved?
- What does she need to hear from you today?

3. The Pyramid Check-In (5 minutes)

Ask yourself:

- Am I operating from safety or survival?
- Am I seeking belonging or betraying myself?
- Am I in Esteem (proving) or Self-actualization (aligning)?

4. Relationship Re-Try Rule (for the healed version of yourself)

If you "try again" you commit to:

- a slow pace
- clear expectations
- one red flag = pause + reality check
- repeating patterns = exit without self-hate

Affirmations for Self-Love + Forgiveness

- I forgive myself for surviving the best way I could.
- I can love people without abandoning myself.
- I do not punish myself for having a heart.
- I am not who I was. I am who I am becoming.
- I rest at the top of the pyramid—I do not live in survival.

Scripture for Reflection

"Above all else, guard your heart..." — Proverbs 4:23

Chapter Twelve

Thriving When Growth Gets Tested

"If you want to fly, you have to give up the things that weigh you down." –Toni Morrison

Keischa woke up late, which meant she was already behind schedule and irritated. Her alarm hadn't gone off. Someone had spilled juice on the couch. Haven couldn't find her shoes. Devin was crying in the bathroom because his favorite shirt was "too scratchy." The coffee maker blinked like it was mocking her. She grabbed for her favorite coffee cup, which slipped from her fingers and crashed to the floor. Dammit. Her chest tightened. Old Keicsha rose up fast. Her body shook. She placed both hands on the counter to steady herself.

"Can EVERYBODY please just shut UP?!!!" she screamed over the noise in her head. Her voice echoed sharply through the kitchen. Silence fell heavy. Haven's face hardened as she froze. Devin's lip trembled.

"I hate this and I hate mornings," Haven whispered under her breath.

And there it was. The look Keischa knew too well, the same one she used to give her own mother. Defeat. Resentment. Smallness. Shame hit immediately. Her nervous system and behavior patterns wanted to barrel forward, fix it, rush, control. That familiar urge to push through, override, survive.

She stopped. Literally stopped moving. She inhaled, slow and deep, the way Traci taught her and began mentally talking herself through the emotions.

"1. Name it: I'm overwhelmed. 2. Locate it: Chest, Jaw. 3. Choose." Keischa settled in, slowed her thoughts, and calmed her mind. She crouched down in front of her kids.

"Okay," she said softly, voice cracking. "Mommy messed up just now." Haven looked surprised and cautious. Devin sniffed as his eyes widened.

"I got angry because I felt rushed," Keischa continued. "But that's not your fault." The room stayed quiet. This was new.

"I'm sorry," she said. "Can we try again?"

Haven nodded slowly. Devin hugged her neck and laughed. "Ok," she said loudly, "Y'all remember our morning chant?"

"Yeah," they said in unison and started singing, "We gotta go... we gotta go."

They were still late. The day was still messy. But something fundamental had shifted. The world didn't come crashing to an end because she couldn't control the circumstances. In this moment, she realized that she had a choice in the outcome. Choice was responsibility, choice was deciding to do something different that repairs relationships.

The kids were barely out of the car before her phone buzzed. It reminded her that she had meant to talk to Traci about why she still felt anxious about the sound of the notifications indicating she had a message. It always came with a twinge of "what now?"

She stared at her reflection in the rearview mirror longer than usual. Her face looked the same, soft brown skin, tired eyes, edges pulled back into a loose bun, but something underneath had shifted. She wasn't bracing for impact the way she used to. Her breath moved all the way into her belly now. Her body didn't feel like it was constantly on standby. The sound of cars and car horns rushing by her at the stoplight rattled her back to reality. She checked her phone out of routine.

"Subject: Quick Turnaround Needed." She already knew what it was. Six months ago Keischa would have opened the email immediately, heart racing, already drafting an apology for whatever boundary she was about to break.

Today, she set the phone face down. The anxiety wasn't completely gone. It had lessened, but she was still shaky. And real talk, she was scared of what was coming. She slowed her breath and forced herself to be in the present. Which meant hitting her playlist and cracking the volume to 1000.

"I'll get to you," she whispered to the email. She reminded herself that the email would still be there once she finished pacing herself and grounded her morning. "Everything isn't a priority", Keischa reminded herself and flowed with the now-moving traffic. "Keischa, you choose you and what's important."

The Choice at Work: Esteem in Real Time

By the time Keischa walked into the conference room, her palms were damp. Old muscle memory and old wiring made her tense.

Her supervisor smiled too tightly. The kind of smile that always came before a request disguised as a compliment.

"We need you to take this on," he said. "You're just so dependable. I know I can count on you." There it was. That word. Dependable. Her nervous system flared, heat rushed to her head and face, her chest tightened.

"Ok, Keisch," she said to herself, *"slow down, ground, count backward. Don't rush to fill the silence."* She felt her feet on the floor. She inhaled slowly, just like Traci had taught her. *"Name the sensation: chest is tight. Breathe. Stay present."*

"I know that this is important," Keischa said evenly. "I want to be honest, up front, about my capacity." The room felt like it was spinning.

"I can do A and B by Friday," she continued, voice steady. "C will need to be reassigned or pushed to next week."

He blinked. "Well, this really needs to be done."

"I understand," she said. "And overextending myself would impact the quality of the work."

Her heart pounded. This was new territory. No over-explaining. No apology. Just truth. Her old self was screaming inside, *"What are you doing? You are going to get fired and then what?"* Then what? Then nothing! She realized she couldn't go back. There was nothing there.

After a long pause, he nodded. "Okay. Let's adjust."

She walked out of the room shaking. Not from fear. From power. Traci's voice rang loudly in her ears as she visualized that pyramid, *"Our friend, Maslow, would call this esteem. Not confidence born from praise, but self-respect rooted in reality."* For the first time, Keischa didn't abandon herself for approval. She chose alignment over attachment.

Keischa

This Sunday felt different to Keischa. The kids were spending the weekend at her mom's house, and she had told Simone after the last workshop that she was going to just chill out this weekend. So, no Saturday visit. And it didn't have anything to do with not wanting to be with her girl.

Keischa lazily walked through the house enjoying the peace and quiet. Her thoughts went to Malcolm. Things had gotten better, but the same ole same ole had still been occurring. Keischa had not talked to Traci about it because, honestly, she felt ashamed, overwhelmed, and stupid. She still made excuses for him after almost two years of dating. She wrote in her journal, "Girl what are you afraid of??!!!

She grabbed her phone to scroll through her feed on Instagram, but decided to check her messages instead. She didn't know what she was looking for. If he had texted or called the phone would have notified her.

"Here we go again," she thought. "The great disappearing act." They had talked about it. She had clearly defined the boundaries and rules to secure healthy attachment so that they could move forward in the relationship. Malcolm had agreed and did everything for a couple of weeks. Then slowly, but surely, he started not answering her calls. He would go hours and days without texting or calling. Keischa laughed out loud and said to no one at all, "Give somebody an inch, they will take a mile."

An hour later, she texted Malcolm. "I've had enough. I'm done." Send. She cried, not because of the hurt, but because of the realization and the truth that choosing herself hurt. It cost her the end of the fantasy.

Malcolm

Malcolm got the text from Keischa saying she was done. He was used to that. He knew whenever she felt neglected, she would lash out. He had tried to explain to her over and over that he needed space, that it had nothing to do with her. He had just agreed to her wants so she would get off his back. He turned up his music and thought, "Here we go again."

And just like that he wasn't thirty-six anymore. He was a child again, sitting at the kitchen table while his parents argued in the next room. His mother's voice was sharp with exhaustion, his father's low and dismissive.

"I'm doing the best I can," his father said.

"That's what you always say," his mother replied. "And then you leave."

Malcolm remembered how his father would disappear after fights, returning days later with apologies that sounded sincere, but changed nothing. Love, in his house, meant enduring disappointment quietly. Wanting more felt dangerous.

He learned early that if you admit you're overwhelmed, you become the problem. If you admit you can't give what's needed, you lose people. Malcolm sat up in his seat, the memory tightened his chest.

He admitted to himself he didn't know how to give Keischa what she was asking for without losing himself in the process. There it was out in the open. Truth.

Keischa

Malcolm's voice note came late at night. Keischa had just finished getting the kids and herself prepared for the upcoming week. The house was settled and she was getting ready to settle in too. She was still feeling uneasy that Malcolm hadn't checked in. Keischa checked her messages one more time, and there it sat: (1) voice memo. She stared at it for what felt like an hour before hitting the play arrow.

"I've been thinking," Malcolm said quietly. No charm. No performance. "I know I disappear when things get real. I watched my dad do that my whole life. I told myself I wouldn't be him and I still didn't learn how to stay." Keischa sat on the edge of the bed, listening.

"I don't want my daughter growing up thinking love feels confusing," he continued. "So, I'm trying to learn how to be present. Even when I'm uncomfortable." He paused. "I'm not asking you for anything. I just needed you to know I see it now."

Keischa didn't cry. She felt sad. Finally, it was clear. During their previous conversations what Malcolm had said seemed like vulnerability and honesty, but it was his way of manipulating her emotions and needs to get what he wanted. That clarity was everything. Her internal response mattered more than his words. She didn't feel pulled. She felt aware.

A few days later, Keischa was sitting and waiting to get out of the drop-off line at the kids' school, it was worse than rush hour traffic, and gave her time to think. The last few weeks had seemed like a whirlwind. She was navigating her new job responsibilities from a big promotion, being a present mommy, and her feelings over the "relationship" with Malcolm. With everything that had been going on Keischa had forgotten to schedule her therapy appointment. She was thinking about when she could get a session in when Simone texted.

"Hey, girlie. Have an amazing day. Call me at lunch. Peace."

Keischa was able to text her back, "Ditto, sis. Talk to you soon."

That text reminded her that it was Wednesday and she still hadn't heard anything from Malcolm since that voice memo on Sunday. She scheduled her therapy appointment for Friday evening and got to work.

Later that evening, she sat in her driveway, willing herself out of her car. She was so grateful that the kids were finally on winter break and staying with their friends. She couldn't have imagined taking care of anyone tonight. She looked in her rearview mirror and saw lights pulling in behind her car. Malcolm. Keischa swallowed. Malcolm knocked softly on the window. Can I get in?

"Yeah," she said reluctantly. She really didn't want to deal with this, but she knew it was happening.

"So...what?" he launched in, "My needs don't matter?"

"They do," she said carefully. "But they don't get to cost me myself anymore."

"That's not fair," he snapped. "I needed more time."

"And I needed consistency," she replied. "We both needed things the other couldn't give."

He shook his head. "You're choosing yourself over us."

"Yes," she said. "I am." Tears burned. This was harder than walking away quietly.

His voice got louder. "You're acting like I'm the villain, when are you going to take accountability for what you do?"

"I'm not saying you are a villain," she said gently, "but I also won't take accountability for things I haven't done. I'm done auditioning for love." That landed.

He softened, then hardened again. "I don't know how to give you what you want."

"I know," she said. "And that's why I have to leave." She cried, tears cascading down her face. Keischa willed them to stop, but they had a mind of their own. The tears fell, not because she doubted herself, but because this time, they both knew it was over. It was real. As Malcolm got out of the car, Keischa heard him say, "Damn," as he slammed the door.

Therapy: Naming the Pattern

Keischa was so ready for this session. Friday evening had taken its sweet time. Keischa needed to unpack a lot of things. Simones's outburst during the self-love workshop, the fear that ran through her speaking up at work, and finally the deep one, Mr. Malcom. Traci's office felt warm and inviting. She breathed in the scents and kicked off her shoes. She smiled slightly at how soft the rug was under her toes and finally curled up on the couch, knees pulled in.

"I ended it," she said in a hurried whisper. Traci didn't rush her.

"With Malcolm." Even saying his name hurt.

"He showed up at the house apologetic," Keischa continued. "Said he was ready now. And for a second, I wanted to believe him. That's why I'm here. I always want to believe him."

Traci nodded. "And what stopped you?"

Keischa exhaled shakily. "My body didn't relax. I realized I'd be negotiating my needs again."

"That's secure awareness," Traci said. "You recognized the anxious-avoidant loop in real time."

They role-played the conversation, creating different endings so Keischa could see how those endings felt in the body and how to hold the boundary she built. The exercise allowed her to see different scenarios and determine that yes, she had chosen what was best for her without betraying her boundaries or introducing punishment. The exercise gave Keischa space for vulnerability, words, and a level of honesty that showed the safety Keischa felt, not only with Traci, but with herself. Tears streamed down Keischa's face.

"I forgive myself," she whispered.

"Let's remember to name it. I forgive myself for..."

Keischa responded slowly and deliberately, "For staying so long."

"That," Traci said gently, "is what we are aiming for. Self-actualization, the moment when survival is no longer your primary identity." This is where you choose what's the best definition of you for yourself. You honor your emotional needs and, my dear, you start to create a life that reflects joy, purpose and self respect." Traci leaned back and let out a giggle. "You chose the best outcome with Malcolm.. What else did you choose recently, that the old you wouldn't have?"

Keischa responded, "Repair instead of performing with Simone. Boundaries instead of appeasement at my job. And pause instead of panic." Traci nodded.

Keischa continued, feeling her strength rise, "I also chose to be good with the outcomes of my decisions. Traci, I just want to confide in you that this whole thriving thing doesn't feel like relief. It feels like responsibility. The responsibility to choose me even when it costs me something."

Traci laughed, "Self-actualization isn't about being perfect or pretending. It's realizing where you hurt and using psychological skills to work on them, so the pain lessens. Picture it like this. We have a white canvas. This canvas represents relationships. If we throw red paint to represent conflict onto the canvas, we know we are never going to get the original white canvas, or "perfect relationship" back."

"But armed with the knowledge of what happened to you and why the relational rupture occurred, you can use the skills you learned to move toward repair. Just like a skilled artist can carefully paint over the red. The goal, for you, is less conflict. The goal, for the artist, becomes to make the canvas less red. The one thing we keep coming back to is making sure you don't abandon yourself. Now, let's get into some breath work, love."

Later that evening, in the quiet of the house Keischa thought about how this year had changed her. Not in big chunks, but in small pieces. Standing in her bathroom brushing her teeth, staring at her own reflection, mouthing the affirmations she wrote on the mirror was so routine it was on autopilot. Her phone buzzed on the counter behind her. She didn't need to look to know who it was. She finished brushing. Rinsed slowly. Dried her hands. Then she picked up the phone.

Malcolm's text read, "I've been thinking about everything you said. I feel like I keep messing this up. Can we talk? I don't want this to be over."

Her chest tightened, not with panic, but with grief. Old Keischa would've responded immediately. Reassured him. Softened the edges of her truth so he wouldn't feel abandoned. She would've said "we'll figure it out" even when she didn't believe it.

Instead, she sat on the edge of the tub and let the feeling move through her without acting on it. She slowly, but deliberately blocked, unblocked, blocked and unblocked him then proceeded to delete his number. That part was just symbolic, she had dialed that number so often she could recite it in her sleep.

Her chest hurt, but it wasn't collapsing. This was the hard work. She thought about Traci's words: *"Self-actualization isn't where attachment disappears. It's where it stops driving the car."* She left out the part of how it feels like the car drove over her, backed up, and drove over her again.

Keischa wondered, *"Am I healed and thriving? This feels like I'm in the basement of that damn pyramid."* She stumbled into the kitchen, poured a glass of wine, and sat in the dark with Sade on a loop before finally dragging herself into the bedroom and crying herself to sleep.

The next morning, Keischa woke before her alarm, sunlight spilling across the bed, her body heavy with emotion, but strangely calm. The old pattern was still there. Yes, she grabbed her phone secretly praying he would have called and begged her to talk to him. Even a good morning text would've been nice.. Something! But nothing was there.

For the first time in a long time, she noticed her pain and longing. She looked out her window and realized that she hadn't spent last night rehearsing conversations or anticipating reactions. She stretched. Her silent phone mocked her. "Damn, Damn, Damn!" she said in her Florida Evans voice. (She loved the old 70s sitcom Good Times.) That line fit perfectly because this breakup felt like a death and in that scene Florida was experiencing a delayed reaction to her grief. Keischa smiled faintly. *"That's crazy. I get it now."*

In the kitchen, she poured coffee and leaned against the counter, letting the quiet settle. Her mind drifted, not to Malcolm, but to a younger version of herself. She saw herself at twenty-seven, sitting in her car outside someone else's apartment, rewriting a text for the fifth time so it wouldn't sound needy. She remembered how she used to shrink her wants into polite suggestions.

She whispered softly to no one and everyone, "I didn't know better." And for the first time, that sentence didn't carry shame. It carried compassion. Simone called.

"You, okay?" Simone asked without preamble. Keischa hesitated then answered honestly.

"Yeah, girl, I'm good. I really broke up with Malcolm. We are done," she said.

Simone exhaled audibly. "Damn."

"It hurts," Keischa admitted. "I still love him."

"Yeah," Simone said gently. "But you didn't abandon you. Check me out getting my therapy language on."

The truth suddenly felt heavy. She hung up assuring Simone she would be back on deck for their Saturday meet-ups. It had been a couple of weeks and she needed her girl-time fix. Alone, before the day kicked in, Keischa placed one hand over her heart and closed her eyes to breathe. She breathed deeply. She spoke slowly, deliberately, letting her body hear the words, "I forgive myself for staying. I forgive myself for hoping. I forgive myself for wanting love. And I choose myself anyway."

Her chest softened. Not because the pain was gone, but because she trusted herself to handle it. That was the meaning of this moment. It was not the end of love. Not the end of longing. It was the end of self-abandonment. And for Keischa, that was everything.

Tools for Thriving

1. The Alignment Question

Ask:"Does this relationship require me to abandon myself for it to survive?"

If yes, it's not self-loving to stay.

2. The Thriving Ladder Check-In

Weekly ask: Where am I operating from—survival, attachment fear, or alignment?

3. The Relapse Plan

When I want to chase, over give, or shrink, I will pause and choose one grounding action.

4. Repair Script

"When this happened, I felt ___. What I need now is ___."

5. Whole-Self Ritual

Create one weekly practice honoring body, boundaries, and belonging.

Affirmations

• I choose alignment over attachment.

• I can grieve what I believed and still grow.

• I am safe to be whole.

• Thriving is allowed to look like me.

Scripture for Reflection

"I have come that they may have life and have it more abundantly." John 10:10

Chapter Thirteen

The Return to Self

"You are your best thing." — Toni Morrison

Keischa

The year hadn't changed Keischa in one big chuck or exciting moment. It wouldn't have shown up as a highlight on Insta. It changed her in a hundred small unglamorous decisions. Small things that nobody talked about. Like how it stopped her from grabbing her phone the second it buzzed. Right now, her phone buzzed on the counter while she adjusted the fluted glasses on her coffee table. Keischa didn't look at the phone. She now let silence sit without treating it like a threat. She started hearing her body before she started defending her heart.

She loved getting ready for her routine Sis Saturday with Simone. It was a comfort she never would have thought she needed. The thought of it made her laugh out loud. Real talk, Keischa never knew there could be this space of safety and trust with another woman. Saturday had become another form of therapy.

She lit her amber and tobacco candle, the wooden wick crackling like a soft clap. The scent filled the room, grounding, earthy, familiar. This was her ritual now. It set the environment, set the tone, and reminded her nervous system it didn't have to sprint. When she picked up her phone, it was on purpose. Two text notifications blinked on the screen.

The first text was from "My Girl", Simone. Her text read, "We celebrating, sis." Keischa had no idea what the celebration was, but she was game.

The second text was from Malcolm. "You going to that workshop again tonight? I saw it on your planner. We need to talk before you go." Her chest tightened so fast it almost felt like the old days. Almost. Because the new version of her noticed the tightening and didn't confuse his request for a command. She read the message again. "We need to talk before you go." That line used to be a leash. Now it was information. She didn't respond. She turned her phone face down. Then, because life loves timing, her doorbell rang.

Simone walked in like she belonged there; hoodie, leggings, hair wrapped, lip gloss on like it mattered. She held a bag of hot wings in one hand and UNO cards in the other like she was delivering medicine. Keischa loved how this settled her emotions. The food, the conversation, the love.

"Happy Saturday, sis," Simone belted out. "It's been a hectic week, girl. These damn dating sites," she said rolling her eyes, "They a mess. These men are all over the place. Imma chill on them for a minute. Anyhow, at this point I need and crave routine." Keischa laughed a real laugh, the kind that startled her because she hadn't forced it.

"Come here," Keischa said, pulling her into a quick hug. Simone's body softened into it like she'd been holding her breath all day.

"You good?" Simone asked, speaking into her shoulder. Keischa hesitated then told the truth.

"Malcolm texted."

Simone pulled back, eyes narrowing like a protective older sister even though she wasn't. "What he have to say?"

Keischa swallowed. "That we need to talk before the workshop."

Simone rolled her eyes so hard it was almost funny. "Boy, not before the workshop. He always trying to get you back into the fog right when you about to breathe."

Keischa sighed. "That's what it feels like."

Simone stared at her, expression softening. "So, what you gon' do?"

Keischa looked around her apartment at her peace, her intentionality, the warm lighting, the candle, the vision board she was building called "My life".

"I'm going to the workshop," she said quietly. "And I'm not rushing. I'm not letting anyone take this away from me."

Simone nodded like she respected that. Then she paused, eyes darting away. "I'm proud of you," she said, almost reluctantly, like the words tasted unfamiliar. "It pisses me off a little."

Keischa blinked. "What?"

Simone waved her hand. "Not like that. It's just… when you change, it forces everybody else to look at what they are still calling normal."

Keischa smiled softly. "You're changing too."

Simone snorted. "I'm trying. And I'm glad Traci decided to add the additional workshop before the next series in the summer. I didn't realize how much I need this space."

They poured mocktails and ate wings standing at the counter, laughing at nothing and everything, the way women do when they're trying not to admit they're scared. When it was time to leave, Simone reached for her keys and paused.

"You feel that?" Simone asked.

Keischa knew exactly what she meant. The invisible line between the old version and the new one.

"Yeah," Keischa whispered. "I feel it."

Simone nodded once, firm. "It feels safe. Damn, girl. How is Traci all up in my head? Let's get out of here and get into this grown woman's work."

The Workshop: Self-Actualization in Real Life

Keischa was so excited and anxious about this workshop. The chairs were always arranged in a wide or semi circle so that they could interact, not classroom rows that seemed stuffy. She loved how the circle said "we're in this together". A circle said "no hiding". Traci stood at the front with her sleeves pushed up, hair in soft curls, eyes steady. Not a performative steadiness. Anchored.

Keischa clocked the details because she always did: the stack of handouts, the markers laid out like tools, Maslow's pyramid drawn on the board with thicker lines than usual. *"Hmm,"* she thought, *"It almost looks aggressive. Like tonight it wasn't drawn to be cute. It was here to tell the truth."*

Women settled into their seats. A woman in a crisp blazer sat with a notebook hugged to her chest like armor. A younger woman with locs kept glancing at the door like she might still run.

An older woman in all black sat upright, lips pressed, eyes sharp like she'd already survived too much to be impressed. Keischa sat between Simone and a woman who introduced herself softly.

"Hey, I'm Nia," she said nervously. "I almost didn't come."

Keischa laughed softly remembering her first time coming to the workshop. Letting it gently wash over her she said out loud, "Girl, I know the feeling."

Traci waited until the room quieted. No rushing. No nervous jokes to soften what needed to be said. "Tonight," Traci began, "we're talking more about self-love and forgiveness as we focus on the level of Self-Actualization."

A few women shifted like their bodies already wanted to argue.

"Not the cute version," Traci added. "Not the meme version. Not the version that fits on a mug."

Someone laughed sharply, not amused. Traci nodded toward the laughter like she welcomed it.

"Self-love is not comfort," she continued. "It's not confidence. It's not manicured peace. It's the ability to stay loyal to yourself when your old patterns start begging for you to come back." She turned to the board and tapped the pyramid.

"We learned early that belonging comes with conditions," Traci continued. "That love is earned. That being needed is the closest thing to being safe. When we incorporate attachment wounds it becomes worse, because when you grow up with inconsistency, your nervous system confuses chaos with connection."

Keischa felt her chest tighten as if her body recognized itself in the room. A woman across the circle raised her hand. She was the older woman in all black, sharp eyes, unshakeable posture.

"I'm Denise," she said. "What if I think all this self-love and self-actualization is something to gain attention, like the kids say 'click bait'. Is this even a real thing? We never talked or needed to talk about this in my day."

The room quieted. It felt like a collective breath was being held .

Traci nodded. "Say more."

Denise's voice didn't tremble, but her hands did. "I've seen sacrifice. I've seen women survive on fumes. I've seen endurance praised like holiness.

But I've never actually seen a Black woman choose herself without paying for it."

Murmurs moved through the circle, agreement, grief, recognition. Simone's breath caught. Keischa felt it beside her like a shift in air. Simone raised her hand before she could talk herself out of it.

"I don't know if there is truth in it either. I mean, I love me, but...when I think about it, what does that even mean? I never had that conversation 'Do you love yourself?' or seen what self-actualization looks like. So yeah, is this a real thing for us, for me." Simone said, voice already cracking.

Heads turned. The room leaned in without meaning to.

"My mom never chose herself," Simone continued. "She stayed tired. Stayed quiet. Stayed responsible. And people called her strong."

Tears slipped down her face like her body had been waiting for years for permission.

"So, when y'all say self-love," Simone whispered, "part of me wants to believe it. But another part of me thinks it's just another fantasy. Like... another thing we're supposed to figure out alone while the world keeps taking from us."

She wiped her cheeks fast, embarrassed by the wetness. "I've never seen it. Ever. I've seen women do for everybody else until there ain't nothing left. I've seen love as labor. I've seen love as suffering."

Simone's voice dropped. "So, when I try to love myself, it feels fake. Like I'm pretending. Like I'm lying. Because if it is real...why doesn't it feel safe?"

The room held her. Not with advice. Not with applause. With presence. Traci stepped into the circle, her face soft, but her posture strong.

"That makes sense," Traci said quietly. "You can't trust what you've never witnessed."

Simone nodded, crying harder now, like those words cracked something open.

Traci turned to the group. "This is why the pyramid matters. Because self-actualization lives higher up. And if your foundation, Safety and Belonging, was unstable, self-actualization will feel like a myth." She paused.

"Attachment wounds make self-love feel unsafe because your body learns that closeness can be taken and love can disappear. So, you cling, or you shut down, or you overperform, or you control. Not because you're broken. Because you adapted."

Traci inhaled slowly. "We sometimes feel like we are going backwards or have failed if we allow ourselves to be human. Understand that thriving isn't a clean sweep. It's an understanding. It's a continual loop of choice. A loop of continually choosing yourself."

"And, listen, we sometimes feel like we have to drain everything from ourselves to prove that we have tried to make something work. We consistently run a race that we are trying to win by ourselves. Then we fall into defeat because we have nothing left. We subconsciously choose the other person by trying to fulfill a need to make them choose us, instead of focusing energy to choose ourselves, " Traci said.

A few women gasped softly. "It's because of what we see, hear, learn, and are taught. The message for us women is always a resounding 'do everything you can do before you care for you,'" she continued.

Her eyes glistened, controlled and honest. "I told myself I was being patient. Understanding. Spiritual. I told myself love requires sacrifice." Traci's voice trembled for the first time. "But the truth? I was betraying myself daily and called it compassion."

The circle was silent in a way that felt sacred.

"I didn't understand that I was desperately giving people what I didn't get as a child, praying that love, compassion, and understanding would return to me. I knew how it felt to need something and not get it," Traci admitted. "So, I stayed where things kept repeating, because at least repetition felt familiar." She looked around at the women, letting them see her. "And one day I realized the relationship wasn't just hurting me. I was hurting me."

Traci swallowed. "I was the one handing myself over."

Keischa's throat tightened. Simone stared at Traci like she was seeing proof that self-love might exist, but it wasn't pretty.

Traci stepped back to the board and wrote one sentence in thick marker: SELF-ACTUALIZATION IS SELF-LOYALTY. Then she turned back to the group. "Tonight, we're doing an exercise," Traci said. "It's called The Return."

She handed out a paper. Three columns were spread across the top: Old Script, What is Cost Me, New Choice. "Write one old script you're tired of repeating," Traci instructed. "Then write what it cost you. Then write the new choice you are committing to."

Pens moved slowly, like people were writing with their whole bodies. Keischa stared at her page– Old script: If I love harder, he'll stay, Cost: My peace. My dignity. My self-trust, New choice: I will not abandon myself to be chosen.

Her hand shook as she wrote it. She wasn't ready to say it out loud. But her body was ready to acknowledge it through writing. Traci opened the floor for sharing. A younger woman about twenty-five with locs and nervous eyes raised her hand.

"I'm Aaliyah," she said. "My old script is... if I set boundaries, people still won't respect them."

Traci nodded. "And what did that cost you?"

Aaliyah's voice cracked. "I stayed with people who already left emotionally."

The room murmured in agreement.

Nia spoke next, quiet but firm. "My old script is... I have to earn rest. Earn love. Earn peace. Cost is, I don't even know who I am when I'm not proving something."

Denise, the woman who asked if self-actualization was real, cleared her throat. "My old script is... if I choose me, I'm selfish," Denise said. "Cost is... I've been tired my whole life."

Traci nodded. "And your new choice?"

Denise inhaled. "My new choice is I'm allowed to be whole."

The room exhaled like they'd been holding their breath for her. Simone sat rigid, eyes red, paper crumpled in her hand. She was so in awe that this woman teaching, poised and educated, had these stories. She stared at Traci like she was living proof that self-love might actually exist, but grateful the story showed it wasn't pretty, structured, or easy.

She raised her hand. Traci didn't push her. She waited. Simone finally whispered, barely audible. "My old script is... pretending."

Traci's voice softened. "And what did it cost you, Simone?"

Simone shook her head like she didn't want to say it. Then she did. "It cost me my confidence. It cost being seen and valued."

Keischa's eyes filled instantly.

Traci stepped toward Simone, voice gentle but unwavering. "And your new choice?"

Simone looked up, tears spilling. "My new choice is... I'm going to try to believe self-love and self-actualization is real even if I've never seen it."

The circle broke. Not with noise, but with emotion, the kind that spreads because it's honest. Somebody reached for Simone's hand. Then another. Then another. Keischa reached too. Simone's fingers clenched around hers like a lifeline. Traci watched them, eyes shining.

"This is what moves us up," Traci said softly. "Not perfection. Not performance. Connection with truth."

The Choice

When Keischa walked out of the workshop, the night air hit her like truth. Cold, clean, undeniable. Simone walked beside her, quiet. Keischa could feel Simone processing—like a heart learning a new language. They reached the parking lot and Simone stopped.

"You, okay?" Simone asked.

Keischa nodded, but it wasn't convincing.

Simone's voice softened. "What's coming up?"

Keischa hesitated.

Then she said the thing she didn't want to admit.

"I'm scared I'm going to go back," she whispered.

Simone blinked. "Back where?"

"Back to chasing," Keischa admitted. "Back to shrinking. Back to apologizing for wanting what I want."

Simone stepped closer. "Then don't."

Keischa laughed once, shaky. "Girl, you make it sound simple."

"It ain't simple," Simone said. "But it is clear."

Keischa's phone buzzed. She didn't have to look. She looked anyway. Malcolm: "I'm outside your place. We need to talk."

Simone's eyes flashed. "He outside?"

Keischa stared at the screen, heart pounding. Old Keischa would've rushed home like she was being summoned. Like love was an emergency. New Keischa took a breath.

"I'm not rushing," she said aloud, mostly to herself.

Simone nodded. "Good."

Keischa typed slowly. "I'm not available tonight. I'll talk tomorrow at 6. If that works."

She hovered over send. She studied the text, held her breath. Deleted it, revised it. Deleted it, went back to the original text, and hit send. Her chest tightened then loosened.

Simone smiled faintly. "Look at you."

Keischa exhaled. "I'm trying."

When Keischa arrived home later, Malcolm was gone. But he had left another message. Malcolm: "So you can make time for everybody else but not me?"

The words hit her body first, heat rising, stomach dropping, that old urge to explain. To prove. To make him understand. Then she remembered her paper from the workshop: Old Script, What it Cost Me, New Choice. She held her phone, trembling. Not because she didn't love him. Because she did. And love used to be where she lost herself.

She sat on the edge of her bathtub, same place she'd sat a hundred times before, negotiating with her own dignity. The candlelight from the living room flickered through the doorway, soft and steady. Keischa placed her hand on her chest.

"Check the body first," Traci's voice echoed in her mind. *"The body remembers before the mind explains."* Her breathing was shallow and quick. She slowed it down with deep breaths. In through the nose. Out through the mouth.

Then she typed, "I'm not making time for everybody else. I'm honoring my capacity." She thought about that for a minute. What did she mean by "honoring her capacity"? Through tears a small voice answered her, *"You no longer have the ability to take in pain, discord, stress. You don't have space for toxic behavior or relationships."*

"Yes", she said out loud and continued typing. "I'm not available to be guilted into connection. If you want to talk, tomorrow at 6 is the time I can offer."

She stared at the message like it was a cliff. Reread it slowly, deleted the last sentence, rewrote it and then she hit send. The moment after was silent. This had always been the scariest place, the ambiguity. Would he be mad? Would he feel like she was doing too much? And the biggest question, would he abandon her by not answering at all? It felt like holding your breath in a space when there was no air available, so you had to conserve it. She heard the sound of her own breathing. And then, unexpectedly, a laugh bubbled up through the tears.

"Girl," she whispered to herself, shaking her head. "Who are you?" A quieter voice answered from inside her chest, *"I'm the one who stays with you."*

Malcolm

Malcolm sat in his car outside Keischa's building, phone in hand, feeling like he was swallowing glass. He wanted it to work. He truly did. He wasn't playing games on purpose. He wasn't trying to control her. He felt helpless. Left behind. Forgotten. Replaceable. He stared at her text on the screen, jaw tightening, "I'm honoring my capacity."

It sounded like rejection, control, like "I don't give a flying fu$k". He reread the word capcity. Girl Wha??? Even her new language was pissing him off. It definitely was because of them workshops. She was never like this before she started getting brainwashed. He rubbed his face hard, frustrated with her, but more frustrated with himself.

"She wants too much," he muttered. But the truth was uglier. She wanted what was healthy. And healthy felt unfamiliar. His mind drifted backward, uninvited. He was eight again, watching his mom fold laundry with swollen eyes while his dad paced the kitchen, keys in hand.

"Why you always on me?" his dad snapped. "I can't breathe in this house. You so damn needy, overbearing."

His mom's voice was quiet, but sharp. "You can breathe. You just don't want to be held accountable." His dad slammed the door and left.

Malcolm remembered the silence after, how his mom would just continue as if nothing had happened. She would straighten the house like cleanliness could fix abandonment. How she never said, "That hurt." How she just kept moving. How she never explained when he asked questions. Just a quick, "I'm ok."

So Malcolm started believing that silence and movement were the keys to not being hurt. When people leave, let them. Don't show them they hurt you. Don't need nobody. If you ask for consistency, you get called controlling. If you feel abandoned, you swallow it. Now here he was, grown, holding his phone like a weapon and a wound. He stared at Keischa's message again. Tomorrow at 6. A boundary.

It felt like the door had been slammed in his face. It felt like she was wielding all the power. His chest hurt. Part of him wanted to punish her for not chasing him. Another part of him wanted to become the kind of man who didn't need her to. He didn't know which part would win. That scared him.

Therapy: The Pivotal Session

The next day, Keischa sat in Traci's office and finally said the sentence she'd been choking on, "I feel stupid. All the work we did this year. Wasted."

Traci didn't blink. She didn't rush to correct her. She let it exist so Keischa could see it clearly. Keischa's eyes filled. "I feel disappointed in myself, in Malcolm, in the whole situation. Like... I should be further along."

Traci's voice was gentle, "Say the thing under that."

Keischa's throat tightened, "I know better. So why do I still want him?"

Traci leaned in, "Because wanting doesn't vanish when you heal."

Keischa shook her head, frustrated. "Then what is self-love? Because if I keep chasing love, do I even love myself?" There it was. The question that haunted so many women, but rarely got spoken out loud. Traci held Keischa's gaze steadily.

"Self-love isn't proven by what you feel," Traci said. "It's revealed by what you choose when what you feel is expensive."

Keischa swallowed, "So... wanting him doesn't mean I don't love myself?"

"No," Traci said firmly. "But chasing him at the cost of your peace would."

Keischa cried hard-ugly revealing her truth. Relieved. Honest. Traci didn't hand her tissues right away. She waited, letting Keischa find her own bottom. When Keischa finally wiped her face, Traci spoke softly, "This stage of the pyramid is tricky," Traci said. "Because belonging and esteem can masquerade as self-actualization. You can look successful and still be emotionally starving. You can feel loved and still be self-abandoning." Keischa nodded, breathing shaky.

"Attachment wounds show up here like a final test," Traci continued. "Not because you're failing, but because your nervous system wants proof you're safe now."

Keischa whispered, "So the test is... can I stay with myself even when I want someone else to stay with me?"

Traci smiled, proud and tender, "That's it."

Keischa leaned back, exhausted, "I'm scared."

Traci's voice softened, "Courage isn't the absence of fear, Keischa. It's fidelity in the presence of it." Keischa wiped her cheeks again.

"And here's what I need you to do," Traci said, jotting something down, then sliding a sheet of paper across the table. "Remember the practice we did at the workshop? Use it again. A thought disappears when something else shows up to take its place."

Keischa looked down at the words: The Return Practice. Yes, she remembered doing this at the workshop. She read the paper, reminding herself of the steps, 1. Name what you want, 2. Name what it costs, 3. Choose what honors you. Keischa stared at the paper like it was a map.

Traci's voice dropped. "This is the next step to thriving. You stop asking 'How do I make this work?' and you start asking 'What honors who I'm becoming?'" Keischa nodded slowly. She wasn't healed. But she was awake. And she trusted awake.

The Conversation

At 6 p.m., Keischa met Malcolm at a quiet café. It was a place that was not romantic or hostile. It was neutral. Intentional. Malcolm walked in looking tired. Not in a victimized way, but in a human way. He sat across from her and exhaled.

"I want this to work," he said quickly. "But it feels like you want more than I can give." Keischa didn't flinch.

Malcolm's jaw tightened. "See? That's what I mean. You're always..." he trailed off. "You always make me feel like I'm failing."

"I'm not trying to make you feel like anything," she replied softly.

"But you do," he admitted, voice rough. "It feels like you're five steps ahead emotionally and I'm always catching up."

Keischa's chest softened. She could feel his sincerity, his fear, his needs. But his words made it sound like she was responsible to care for those needs. And she could feel her own center honoring her responsibility to herself.

"I don't need you to be five steps ahead," she said gently. "I need you to stop making my boundaries feel like rejection."

Malcolm looked away, frustrated. "When you pull back, I feel like I'm about to lose you."

Keischa's heart thumped. There it was again. The pattern. The invitation to reassure. To shrink. To make him comfortable at her expense. Keischa placed her hand on the table, grounding herself.

"I'm going to say this clearly," she said. "When you say that, my body goes into fix-it mode. And I'm not doing that anymore."

Malcolm's eyes widened slightly. "So, now I can't tell you how I feel? It's all about you."

"You can," she replied. "But not at the expense of me. Your feelings are yours to manage.

He swallowed, struggling. He felt his pride rising and his ego saying, *"You the man who she talking to?"*

Keischa's voice softened, not to rescue him, but to stay humane. "I care about you. I do. But I'm not available for guilt, pressure, or emotional punishment when I honor my capacity."

Malcolm's face tightened. "So, what are you saying?"

Keischa inhaled slowly. "I'm saying I'm stepping back," she said. "Not because I don't care. Because I do. I'm learning to care about me."

Malcolm stared at her, pain and frustration warring in his expression. "You're choosing you," he whispered, like the words tasted bitter.

Keischa nodded. "Yes." Silence held them.

Then Malcolm exhaled, voice low. "I hate that it feels like you're leaving."

Keischa's eyes filled, but her spine stayed straight. "I'm not leaving to punish you," she said. "I'm leaving to stop punishing myself."

Malcolm blinked rapidly, like he didn't want her to see the water in his eyes. "Okay," he whispered.

It wasn't closure. But it was truth. And truth was enough.

Family, Kids, and the Old Pull

Keischa didn't go home after the café. Not right away. She sat in her car for a minute with her hands on the steering wheel, breathing like she'd run up a hill. Her phone was silent, too silent. The kind of silence that used to make her spiral. Then it buzzed. *"That's what you get for putting that into the universe"* she thought, as she read "School: Reminder: Spirit Week tomorrow. Pajama Day."

Keischa stared at the message and laughed, short and watery. Of course. Of course, the universe would follow her grown woman heartbreak moment with pajamas and snacks and permission slips. She wiped her face with the back of her hand and whispered, "Okay. I'm still a mom."

When she picked the kids up from her mother's, they barreled into the car with backpacks too big for their bodies and voices too loud for her nervous system.

"Mommyyyyy," her youngest, Devin, sang out climbing in like he owned the place. "We need pajamas tomorrow and I told my teacher we got the good ones."

Keischa glanced at him in the mirror. "You told her I had the good ones?" she asked quizzically.

He nodded like it was obvious. "Yeah. Because you always come through with the good stuff."

That hit her in the chest. She didn't realize he noticed that she always went over and above to get them nice things. In the backseat her oldest, Haven, was quiet. Headphones on, but not playing anything. Keischa recognized that stillness. She used to wear it too. "You good?" she asked softly.

Haven shrugged without looking up. "Yeah." Keischa waited.

Haven shifted and finally said, "You been sad. What happened?"

Keischa didn't deny it. She didn't lie to protect them from the truth. She had learned that lesson too. Kids feel what you don't name, and then they blame themselves for it. "I've been going through something," she said gently. "But I'm okay. I'm taking care of myself."

Haven nodded once like she respected that. After a moment she added, "Is that why you been going to them meetings?"

Keischa smiled. "The workshops?"

"Yeah," she said. "Simone be saying you in healing school."

Keischa laughed. "Simone is dramatic."

Haven cracked a tiny smile. "So, when are you graduating?"

Keischa glanced at her smiling, reacting to her beauty, heart full. "I'm learning," she said. "And learning counts."

Haven leaned back, the conversation was over, but the air in the car felt different. Like safety had been named. Like her kids could relax because she was honest and not pretending. At home, Keischa moved through the evening like a woman holding two truths at once.

She helped with homework, heated leftovers, found the "good pajamas." Then signed the form she forgot was due today, refilled the water bottles, smiled at the same jokes, and sat through the same story about the same friend at lunch.

And every time she felt the ache rise, remembering Malcolm at the café and the end of their relationship, she busied herself and did something new. She didn't swallow it. She didn't drown in it. She touched her chest lightly and whispered, "I'm here."

After the kids were finally settled for the evening, teeth brushed, prayers prayed, night lights glowing, Keischa stood at her sink rinsing a cup, letting the warm water run longer than needed. Her phone buzzed again. This time, her stomach dropped before she even looked. Rayna. Keischa stared at the name like it was a ghost with a cash app request.

Rayna. How did she get through? She thought she had blocked her. Keischa thought that last text had said what needed to be said. What was this? She was scared to open it. Her stomach was in knots as she gripped the phone tightly.

Rayna had a way of bringing Keischa back to her thirteen-year-old self. It pulled her into a mental space that made her feel wrong and obligated. Where she couldn't say "no" and felt helpless against Rayna's manipulation and bullying. A space where she didn't feel she had the right not to be loyal. She didn't feel safe.

Keischa dried her hands slowly before opening the message, "Hey, cousin. I been meaning to call you back. I don't like how we ended things. We fam, cuz. You good? I miss you."

Keischa's chest tightened because the message looked like love, but Keischa had learned: sometimes love is just a softer entry point for dysfunction. She didn't respond right away. She sat down on the couch with a candle burning. The smell of amber and tobacco had a calming effect, the wooden wick crackling steaded her heartbeat.

Then the second message came, "Also... I'm in a lil jam. I need to borrow $300 until Friday. Please don't make it a thing. You know how you can get. I don't need that energy right now."

There it was. Keischa leaned her head back, eyes closing. The old version of her would have sent it immediately. Not because she wanted to, but because she didn't want to deal with the guilt.

Because family disappointment felt like abandonment. Because saying no felt like she was betraying the role she was born into: the dependable one. Her body tried to sprint into explanation. She started texting, "I'm sorry. I wish I could. I'm stretched. I'm dealing with things. I've got bills and things the kids need. I don't mean no..."

Delete. *"No, that's not it,"* Keischa thought. She closed her eyes and breathed deeply. Keischa opened her eyes. Traci's voice echoed in her mind,

"Self-actualization is self-loyalty." She looked at the quiet hallway where her kids slept. Her kids didn't need a martyr. They needed a mother who knew how to protect peace and resources without shame. Keischa typed slowly, hands steady even though her heart wasn't.

"Hey, Rayna. I hear you. I'm not able to lend money right now. I hope you're able to work it out. If you want to talk, I'm here." Keischa stared at the message. It felt too clean. Too firm. Too grown. It felt like freedom. It also felt foreign and scary. She hit send. The response came fast, of course it did.

Rayna's words sprung at her like a slap, "Wow. Okay. I see how it is. You've changed. Everybody changing and forgetting who held them down."

Keischa felt the sting. Old Keischa would have folded, just to prove she wasn't selfish. New Keischa noticed the sting and didn't translate it into obligation. She didn't argue. She didn't defend. She didn't write a paragraph auditioning to be understood. She placed her phone face down. And whispered, steady and soft, "I can love you and still say no."

Her eyes watered, not because she regretted it, but because she was finally seeing the pattern for what it was. Rayna wasn't asking for connection. She was asking for access. Keischa sat back, letting the silence settle. Then she laughed, a little incredulous, like she couldn't believe she just did that.

"Look at me," she whispered. "Out here acting like I'm healed." The candle crackled. The apartment held her. And for the first time in her life, Keischa didn't confuse family backlash with failure. She knew what it was. A test. And she passed.

Sisterhood

That night, Simone came over without texting first, carrying a bag of chips and two ginger ales like a woman on a mission. Keischa opened the door and Simone didn't ask questions, she just pulled her into a hug. Keischa broke immediately. Not pretty. Not controlled. Simone held her like she'd practiced. When Keischa finally pulled back, her face swollen, Simone squinted at her.

"You look like you been fighting for your life," Simone said.

Keischa laughed through tears, "It felt like it."

Simone nodded, "Because you were."

They sat on the kitchen floor like teenagers, like sisters. Keischa told her everything, and Simone listened without trying to fix it. When Keischa finished, Simone leaned her head on Keischa's shoulder, "Damn, girl, I thought I was going through it." Laughing nervously she added, "I'm glad you hold me down. And, real talk, that I'm Single single." They burst out in laughter. Then Simone said with a somber voice and spirit, "Sis, real talk, I'm proud of you."

Keischa sniffed, "You said that last week."

Simone sighed dramatically, "I'm saying it again. Repetition is healing."

Keischa laughed for real then, the sound surprising both of them. Simone sat up, wiping her own eyes like she didn't want attention.

"You know what's wild?" Simone whispered. "Watching you choose yourself makes me mad and hopeful at the same time."

Keischa tilted her head, "Mad?"

Simone nodded, "Because it shows me I can't keep pretending self-love and self-actualization don't exist."

Her voice dropped, "I said that in the workshop and meant it. I've never seen it. Not in my house, not in my family. But... I saw it today." Keischa's throat tightened.

Simone looked at her, eyes fierce and soft, "So, if it's real for you... maybe it can be real for me too."

Keischa reached for her hand, "It can."

Simone sniffed, "Don't start being inspirational right now."

Keischa laughed, "Girl, hush."

They sat there for a moment, quiet. Then Simone grabbed the UNO cards.

"Now," she said, cracking her knuckles, "I'm about to humble you with my gaming skills, growth, and expertise. Before we get started, what you got on my 40, homie?"

"Girl, what??!" Keischa laughed so hard she had to wipe her eyes again.

"Yeah," Simone said with confidence, "if I'm 'bout to put this whipping on you we gon' need something stronger than ginger ale."

This was the miracle too. Not just in the leaving and learning. In the living.

The Year in One Breath

Later, after Simone left, Keischa stood at her window. The candle still burning behind her, the city hummed below unbothered, alive, moving forward. She realized the world goes on whether she was stretched out under it or sitting on top. She placed one hand over her heart. Not to quiet it. To honor it. Twelve months ago, she would've called this loneliness. Now, she knew it was space.

Space to hear herself. Space to return to herself. Space to become who she was always meant to be, before the world taught her love meant earning. She whispered into the dark, "I am my best thing." It didn't sound like a goal. It sounded like truth.

Becoming

When Keischa reached this place of inner calm, nothing in her life had magically resolved. Some relationships were still complicated. Some answers still hadn't come. What changed was not her circumstances, it was her orientation to herself.

For most of her life, Keischa had moved through the world trying to secure safety through performance. If she was strong enough, accommodating enough, useful enough, maybe she wouldn't be left. Maybe she wouldn't be disappointed. Maybe she could outrun the quiet fear that she was "too much" and "not enough" at the same time.

Therapy didn't erase those fears. It gave her the ability to recognize them as signals, instead of commands. Therapy did not give Keischa a new personality. It gave her language. It gave her awareness. It gave her the ability to trace her reactions back to their roots, instead of judging herself for having them. For the first time, she understood why she did what she did. That understanding changed everything.

She understood how early experiences shaped the way she attached, how unmet needs taught her to over-function, over-give, and stay silent when something didn't feel right. What once felt like personal failure, revealed itself as adaptation. She wasn't broken, she was responding exactly as she had learned to. And with that understanding came a harder kind of growth.

There were moments when Keischa felt the pull to return to what was familiar. Moments when clarity would have required confrontation. When rest felt irresponsible. When choosing herself meant disappointing someone who was used to her availability. In the past, she would have explained herself. She would have chased reassurance. She would have negotiated her needs down to something more acceptable that people could digest and tolerate.

Growth didn't mean she stopped needing people. It meant she stopped disappearing in order to keep them. She learned that love does not require self-abandonment. That boundaries are not walls, but bridges to healthier connections. That choosing herself did not mean being alone, it meant being present. Present in her body. Present in her choices. Present in her relationships.

And slowly, the way she showed up began to change. She began to move up the pyramid. Not in ambition, but in alignment. From survival to stability. From longing to connection. From constantly reaching outward to finally reaching inward, trusting herself. This wasn't a destination. It was a pattern interruption. A new way of relating to others and to herself.

If you recognize yourself in Keischa, it's because your patterns also make sense. Many Black women were taught to be resilient before they were allowed to be supported, were needed before they were nurtured, and praised for holding everything together while quietly learning that their needs were inconvenient. What helped you survive then, may now be exhausting. And exhaustion is not a personal failing. It is information.

This work is not about becoming someone new. It is about understanding why you do what you do, how you show up in relationships, and what changes when you no longer abandon yourself to stay connected.

You may not leave the journey of this story with every answer, but you now have something far more powerful: awareness. You can notice when your body signals unsafety. You can recognize when attachment pulls you toward familiarity instead of wellness. You can locate your unmet needs without shame and meet them with intention.

That is what growth looks like. It is quieter than we expected. Slower. Less performative. It does not announce itself. It shows up in the moments you pause instead of pursuing. In the boundary you hold without explaining. In the choice to rest even when no one claps for it.

This is what *I Close My Eyes to Breathe* has always meant. Not escaping your life, but staying present in it. Creating space between impulse and choice. Trusting yourself enough to remain. This is not the end of your healing, but it is the end of doing it in survival mode.

Once you understand what has been driving you—once you learn how safety, attachment, and unmet needs have shaped your story– you are no longer just surviving it, you are participating in it. And that changes how everything unfolds. Before you close this book, pause, breathe, and read this slowly, "Beloved, I wish above all things that thou mayest prosper and be in health, even as thy soul prospereth" -3 John 1:2

Supportive Tools for the Reader: The Return to Yourself

1) The Pyramid Check-In

Ask yourself weekly:

- What level am I living from —Safety, Belonging, Esteem, or Self-actualization?
- What triggered me downward?
- What helps me return upward without self-abandonment?

Remember: You can go up and down the levels. Growth is returning, not arriving.

2) The Return Practice

1. Name what you want.
2. Name what it costs.
3. Choose what honors you.

Wanting isn't the problem. Betraying yourself to keep it is.

3) Boundary Script for Emotional Pressure

Use these phrases when someone tries to guilt you into connection:

"I care about you. And I'm honoring my capacity."

"I'm not available for guilt or pressure."

"If you want to talk, here's what I can offer."

4) Self-Forgiveness Script (for the "I feel stupid" days)

Say or write:

"I forgive myself for surviving the best way I knew how."

"I forgive myself for staying too long."

"I honor the woman who knows more now."

Affirmations

- I do not abandon myself to be chosen.
- My needs are not inconvenient.
- I can love without losing my center.
- Discomfort is not dangerous.
- Self-actualization is self-loyalty.

Scripture for Reflection

"See, I am doing a new thing! Now it springs up; do you not perceive it?"— Isaiah 43:19

Chapter Fourteen

Acknowlegements

This book was shaped by both scholarship and spirit.

My understanding of human connection is grounded in the foundational work of John Bowlby (1969) and Mary Ainsworth et al. (1978), whose research in Attachment Theory illuminated how early bonds shape emotional development across the lifespan.

The structural framework of this work is informed by Abraham H. Maslow's (1943) Theory of Human Motivation and the Hierarchy of Needs, which articulates the layered movement from physiological survival toward belonging, esteem, and ultimately, self-actualization.

Research on stress, coping, and resilience by Matheny and colleagues (1986) further contributes to the psychological lens woven throughout these pages.

I also acknowledge the scholarship of Dr. Rudolph H. Guess, and others, committed to culturally grounded psychological practice that centers lived experience, identity, and context.

Spiritually, this book is anchored in the Holy Bible, King James Version (public domain).

I would be remiss if I didn't hug the neck of Dr. Lynnette Adams for always picking up the phone, validating me, and showing how the journey of Keischa mirrored her own.

Thank you to Kyarra Jones, who could probably read the book back to me, for her allowing me to remember that what I do doesn't have to reach the masses, my work matters to one person, and it changed her life.

From Black feminist and liberation scholarship, I honor:

Audre Lorde, whose work framed self-care as an act of preservation and political resistance (*A Burst of Light*, 1988).

Dr. Martin Luther King Jr., who taught that faith often requires courageous action before clarity (*The Three Dimensions of a Complete Life*, 1962).

Ntozake Shange, whose writing invited women to locate the divine within themselves (*For Colored Girls Who Have Considered Suicide / When the Rainbow Is Enuf*, 1975).

I acknowledge Angela Davis for her scholarship on race, gender, and liberation, Toni Morrison for her enduring literary legacy that centered Black interior life, and Tricia Hersey, founder of The Nap Ministry, for reframing rest as a form of resistance (*Rest Is Resistance*, 2022).

To the artistry of Anita Baker, whose music has accompanied many seasons of healing — thank you.

Above all, I give gratitude to God who rejoices over us with singing (Zephaniah 3:17, KJV).

References

Scripture quotations are from the King James Version (KJV), which is in the public domain.

All referenced works are cited for scholarly and educational purposes. No copyrighted literary passages, lyrics, or protected text are reproduced in full. All rights to referenced works remain with their respective authors, estates, and publishers.

Ainsworth, M. D. S., Blehar, M. C., Waters, E., & Wall, S. (1978). *Patterns of attachment.* Lawrence Erlbaum.

Bowlby, J. (1969). *Attachment and loss: Vol. 1. Attachment.* Basic Books.

King, M. L., Jr. (1962). *The Three Dimensions of a Complete Life.* Sermon, Ebenezer Baptist Church.

Lorde, A. (1988). *A Burst of Light.* Firebrand Books.

Maslow, A. H. (1943). A theory of human motivation. *Psychological Review, 50*(4), 370–396.

Matheny, K. B., Aycock, D. W., Pugh, J. L., Curlette, W. L., & Silva Cannella, K. A. (1986). Stress coping: A qualitative and quantitative synthesis. *Journal of Clinical Psychology, 42*(4), 499–507.

Shange, N. (1975). *For Colored Girls Who Have Considered Suicide / When the Rainbow Is Enuf.* Macmillan.

Hersey, T. (2022). *Rest Is Resistance: A Manifesto.* Little, Brown Spark.

Davis, A. (1983). *Women, Race & Class.* Random House.

Morrison, T. (1993). Nobel Lecture.

"For thou shalt go to all that I shall send thee..." *Jeremiah 1:7 (KJV)*

"And he shall be like a tree planted by the rivers of water..." *Psalm 1:3 (KJV)*

"The Lord thy God in the midst of thee is mighty... he will rejoice over thee with joy." *Zephaniah 3:17 (KJV)*

"My grace is sufficient for thee: for my strength is made perfect in weakness." *2 Corinthians 12:9 (KJV)*

"Come unto me, all ye that labour and are heavy laden..." *Matthew 11:28 (KJV)*

"Keep thy heart with all diligence; for out of it are the issues of life." *Proverbs 4:23 (KJV)*